# Emperor Ofcom's new clothes

How the market approach to radio spectrum
failed the country's mobile infrastructure and
how to turn it around

*By* Professor Stephen Temple and
Professor William Webb

ISBN: 9798868007750

First published January 2024

# Preface

For the past twenty years the UK's revolutionary market approach to mobile spectrum regulation has divided views into two parallel universes. In one universe is Ofcom. They have believed in tools based upon the economic theory of a market approach. In the other universe are the UK's Mobile Network Operators who sometimes despair at the tools themselves or how they have been used. Sitting above both are Government officials who have been disappointed, more often than not, at the underwhelming outcomes in achieving national wireless infrastructure goals. No single person exists that has both the depth of expertise and the complete picture to work out what has been going wrong and why.

That is why this book is so unique. We both have deep spectrum expertise. But each of us comes from a different universe and poles apart in our associated beliefs. One of us was an ex-Ofcom official who led the Ofcom Spectrum Framework Review in 2004 that resulted in Ofcom embracing the market approach. The other was, at the time, a director in the corporate strategy group of a mobile network operator and earlier a DTI senior official who had largely shaped the government's 2G mobile spectrum release approach. This meant that our forensic examination led us to look at the same evidence though quite different lenses. It resulted in explosive Zoom meetings that peeled away our pre-conceived views. The result is the nearest anyone will come to the truth of why the market approach to licensed mobile spectrum has failed to achieve any of its objectives.

Our initial intention for the second half of the book was to float a hypothesis of what might replace the failed market approach. Improving the quality of universal mobile coverage looked promising. We were open to other possibilities Then we came to realise that there were no other possibilities for securing more economically efficient use for mobile spectrum that is now inextricably tied into a critical national infrastructure.

As we pieced together what the new revolutionary approach had to look like, many of the pieces just fell into place. For example, there had to be far better alignment between the national infrastructure goals set by the Government and how Ofcom were applying its regulatory spectrum tools. We arrived at a revolution that supports a government setting ambitious goals for improving the essential quality of coverage universally (without needing a substantial taxpayer subsidy) and unchains Ofcom from a past financial extractive approach, leaving them better able to fashion a pro-investment regulatory framework within which mobile network operators could more readily find *a profitable path* to successfully delivering those goals.

Just when we thought the job was done, we asked two people with huge experience in wireless regulation and competition policy to peer review our efforts. It brought a second infusion of intellectual insights. For this we are both extremely grateful.


Stephen Temple
William Webb
January 2024

# Contents

# Contents

## List of abbreviations

| | |
|---|---|
| 1G – 5G | Generations of mobile technology |
| AI | Artificial Intelligence |
| AR | Augmented Reality |
| ALF | Annual Licence Fees |
| CBRS | Citizens Broadband Radio Service |
| CEO | Chief Executive Officer |
| DSA | Dynamic Spectrum Access |
| DSIT | Department of Science, Innovation and Technology |
| DTH | Direct To Handset |
| DTI | Department of Trade and Industry |
| DTT | Digital Terrestrial Television |
| FDD | Frequency Division Duplex |
| GAA | General Authorised Access |
| GDP | Gross Domestic Product |
| GSM | Global System for Mobile communications |
| HAPs | High Altitude Platforms |
| ITU | International Telecommunications Union |
| LEO | Low Earth Orbit (satellite) |
| LSA | Licensed Shared Access |
| MNO | Mobile Network Operator |
| MoD | Ministry of Defence |
| PAL | Priority Access Licence |
| QoS | Quality of Service |
| SMS | Short Message Service |
| SRN | Shared Rural Network |
| SUR | Spectrum Usage Right |
| TDD | Time Division Duplex |
| TVWS | TV White Space |
| VR | Virtual Reality |

# 1 Introduction

## *1.1 Legacy of a poor quality of universal mobile coverage*

A White Paper from the University of Surrey[1] on mobile regulation noted that 40 years since the first cellular mobile call in the UK:

- Basic connectivity is not yet everywhere, with many gaps on transport routes and in "not spots".
- The Shared Rural Network has a poor "universal speed" specification (90% probability of 2 Mb/s down and nothing guaranteed up) and many lengths of rural roads with no mobile coverage at all.
- A population greater than that of Denmark or Ireland is being left ever further behind in their quality of mobile coverage (the new digital divide).
- Much of the country is dependent upon "narrow bandwidth" 4G or 5G, where the data capacity is insufficient for the likely increase in demand as we move to autonomous cars and similar.
- Wide-bandwidth mobile service, on its current trajectory, will only reach around a third of the UK.

There are several important contributory factors to this poor infrastructure outcome. This book focusses on the role the mobile regulatory framework has played. There is a particular focus on what is called "the market approach" to spectrum management. By the market approach we mean the belief[2] that markets are better at putting spectrum into the hands of the optimal users than regulators or governments. This implies the ability of users to re-purpose and trade spectrum between them and ideally leads to a situation where no regulatory involvement in licensed spectrum is needed.

---

[1]  See  https://www.surrey.ac.uk/sites/default/files/2023-11/from-patchy-to-powerful-white-paper.pdf

[2] This was set out most famously in the Coase Theory which says that the initial distribution of licences is unimportant as long as property rights are well defined, and trading is unimpeded.

This approach has been applied to licensed mobile spectrum over the past twenty years, primarily in the form of auctions and annual licence fees. Their particular design, driven by the market approach to spectrum, has had a detrimental impact:

1. It is heavily financially extractive, and this is unhelpful in today's situation where (for other reasons) the mobile network operators find themselves with a depleted capacity to invest and, in addition, prospects of significant taxpayer funding to redress market failures are also limited.
2. It results in a somewhat hands-off approach, where regulatory input cannot be directed towards meeting the broader needs of the country and has had a haphazard impact on the quality of the infrastructure.
3. It blocks a more productive use of spectrum policy tools to improve the economics of continuously upgrading the universal essential quality of coverage of our mobile networks.

## 1.2  Diagnosing the problems with the market approach

What distinguishes licensed mobile spectrum, because of the market approach, is the huge price barrier to entry to using the spectrum as shown below.

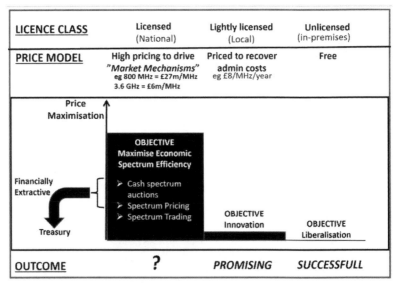

Figure 1– The prevailing landscape over the past 20 years

This high price is the result of cash spectrum auctions and expensive annual licence fees for spectrum acquired before spectrum auctions. The intended purpose of this financially extractive approach has been to drive up economic spectrum efficiency by putting the spectrum into the hands of those who would, in theory, make the most productive use of it for the country.

Part 1 of the book shows in some detail why the claimed economic spectrum efficiency benefits have not materialised. It reveals that the market approach was never applied correctly and that we have something closer to command & control with high fees which in no way aligns with the Coase Theory[3] or other underlying market mechanism philosophies. It shows how the unpredictability of those parts of the market approach that were applied – primarily auctions - has had an unintended consequence on the quality of coverage of our national mobile networks. It explains why the financially extractive nature of the approach is singularly unhelpful as much investment is still needed but both private and public investment are now in short supply.

## *1.3   What a better approach looks like for the next 20 years*

Part 2 shows that what does make sense is for Ofcom to pull its regulatory policy levers to improve the essential quality of what has become a UK critical infrastructure. It is demonstrated that such an infrastructure quality led spectrum policy is a better means (in fact the only means) of driving up economic spectrum efficiency.

This new approach is illustrated in Figure 2.

Part 2 gives a number of illustrative examples of how a network's essential quality of coverage might be improved under the four headings shown inside the black box in Figure 2. By "Essential Quality of Coverage" we mean that there are not only basic mobile connections available but also sufficient data capacity

---

[3] We will explain this in more detail later, but broadly the theory states that it does not matter who gets the original licenses as long as the property rights are well defined, and trading can easily happen. The market will then sort out the best resolution to disputes and ownership.

to support all concurrent active users and their applications, ensuring each user experience is seamless and uninterrupted.

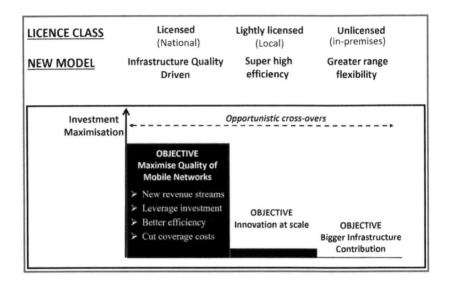

Figure 2– Making a success of what licensed mobile spectrum is being used for today

Necessary for this new approach is a rebalance of policy power between the Government and Ofcom. Here the role of the Government is to set the infrastructure goals for an independent Ofcom to work out how best to deliver them.

This new approach also must take into account that mobile *infrastructure*[4] competition is now weak and cannot be relied upon to drive investment and innovation. This motivational gap must be filled by a far greater extent of cooperation between MNOs to achieve much higher spectrum and quality of coverage efficiencies. This will take time and a mindset change. The outcome

---

[4] Here we distinguish between price competition to deliver the lowest cost service, which remains strong, and infrastructure competition to deliver the highest quality network which we content is weak.

will be a new consensus between the government, Ofcom, and MNOs on the optimal boundary between competition, regulation, and cooperation.

Also shown in Figure 2 is how the lightly licensed and unlicensed spectrum can be made a part of the "better national infrastructure" story without compromising their separate objectives. There are specific chapters for each of these in Part 2.

## 1.4 The Long-Term Future

In the final chapter of the book, we show very briefly where spectrum management may arrive in a world of enormous computing power and artificial intelligence (AI).

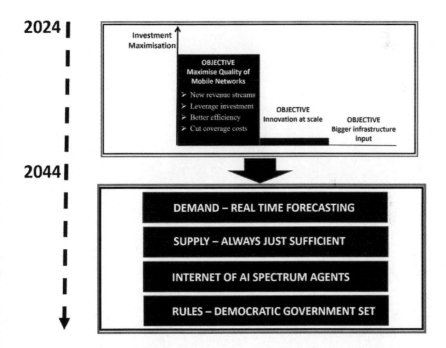

Figure 3– What spectrum management may look like in the distant future

Whilst trying to predict 20 years out is generally a matter of visionary opinion, it seems highly likely that AI will play a significant role as the complexity builds up from the densification of spectrum sharing. However, the wide diffusion of

AI into spectrum management calls into question who is setting the priorities for its use? Our new approach, where an elected government sets the overall goals and national priorities, would position the UK to be more confident in embracing the wide deployment of AI in spectrum management.

Whilst the book focusses entirely on the UK, many of the shortcomings are shared by several countries in Europe and the rest of the world that also embraced the market approach principles to their spectrum policy. All these countries (and many more) share the same future challenges as the UK and there is a huge mutual upside in finding common regulatory solutions that generate scale economies to the benefit of all.

# Part 1

# Why the market approach to spectrum did not work as hoped

# 2 Have Spectrum Auctions achieved their goals?

The spectrum auction has become Ofcom's default approach to releasing spectrum for mobile use. There are other approaches to spectrum releases that, in specific circumstances, could achieve a far better more targeted outcome. We come to some of these in Part 2.

Spectrum auctions are designed to achieve the regulator's specific policy goals. Thus, not all spectrum auctions are the same, with different designs to achieve different policy goals. The following have been quoted in the literature as the various goals:

1. Making the most economically efficient use of the spectrum.
2. A means to maximise mobile coverage.
3. Timely way to release new spectrum onto the market.
4. Effective and transparent means to secure new market entry.
5. Raising the maximum amount of money for the Treasury.

From the above list the first is the one that has been Ofcom's principal policy goal. The second has arisen when Ofcom tries to also achieve a coverage goal. The third is a claim made for the advantage of spectrum auctions in general. The fourth is quite pivotal given the barriers to new market entry. The final one has never been a policy goal of Ofcom but has been a significant benefit for the Treasury. It has been how the media and public judge the success of a spectrum auction.

## 2.1 Making the most economically efficient use of the spectrum

Economic spectrum efficiency is Ofcom's primary goal. Auction theory says that the party willing to pay the most for the spectrum at an auction must have the most productive use and therefore maximises the economic value to the country. Ofcom has embraced this theory as the best means of maximising economic efficiency of mobile spectrum. The cost to the industry so far from this approach has been enormous (around £27.5 billion in auction fees) and we will show later that the approach has also created collateral damage to the nation's mobile infrastructure. It is therefore very important to know if the theory works in practice and really does deliver better economic spectrum efficiency. There can be three outcomes to our investigation: that a cause-and-effect link can be proved (billions of pounds of economic spectrum efficiency gains are visible), or the link is problematic and the gains invisible, or that the link does not exist at all.

In business nobody usually invests in an asset without the prospect of that investment paying back with profit in a reasonable time. This general truth has been carried across to mobile spectrum. The highest bid price is assumed to rest on a business case for an investment in the most profitable use for the bidder. This maximises the economic benefit to the country.

Let's take an illustrative example of a spectrum auction for a new mobile broadband network:

|  | Intended coverage of the UK population | Mobile subsidy to stimulate growth | Target customer size | Bid size | National benefit |
|---|---|---|---|---|---|
| Bidder A | Just M25 | Low | 1m | Low | Low |
| Bidder B | 70% of the population | Medium | 2.5m | Medium | Medium |
| Bidder C | 90% of the population | High | 10m | High | High |

Table 1 – Example spectrum auction

Bidder C can place the highest bid as their business case is to invest to create a 10 million customer base. Bidder A is not happy to tie-up capital for so long before seeing a return. They see just covering London out to the M25 requiring the least capital and the fastest payback. But a customer base of only 1 million limits the size of their bid to being low. Bidder B has a business case somewhere between the other two. Bidder C wins the spectrum, invests the most, creates more jobs in the process and delivers more benefits to more people over more of the country. The auction has delivered the most economically efficient use of that spectrum for the country.

That seems to work well in theory, but does it work in practice? Since the regulator does not vet the bidders' intentions, it is not certain that the high bidder has that high investment intention and, even if they had on the day of the auction, what assurance do they have that it is followed through with? There is also a bit of a leap in assuming that a bidder maximising their own profit equates to the country maximising the economic (and societal) value from the use of that spectrum.

In fact, the theory has three major fallacies:

1. The intentions of the bidder for the most productive use are never made a condition of the spectrum licence. Intentions change (as will be shown below).
2. It is not always "the most productive use" that drives auction prices.
3. Substantial mobile network externalities means that there is no longer alignment of MNOs' most productive use (to them) and the most productive use for the country of the spectrum.

## 2.1.1 The highest bid price equates to the most productive use of the spectrum

This is a fundamentally important assumption that might hold true at the time of bidding but intended uses invariably change over time. No regulator ever turns the highest bidders intended "most productive use" into a contract condition in their licence for the spectrum. In fact, regulators do not even ask what the spectrum is to be used for or any evidence of the projected benefits from its use.

Where companies have the freedom to change their intentions they can and will in response to changing market conditions, changing corporate strategies, and changing technology. Table 2 provides the evidence of this in what followed the 3G auction:

| Year | Events |
|------|--------|
| 2000 | France Telecom acquires Orange |
| 2000 | New CEO of EE (then Orange) Solomon Trujillo |
| 2001 | BT Wireless demerged from BT Group to became O2 |
| 2001 | New CEO of O2 Peter Erskine |
| 2003 | New CEO of EE (then Orange) Jean-Francois Pontal |
| 2003 | New CEO of Three Bob Fuller |
| 2003 | New CEO of Vodafone Arun Sarin |
| 2003 | 3G technology release 99 seriously underperforms |
| 2003 | Skype first appears |
| 2004 | New CEO of EE (then Orange) Sanjiv Ahuja |
| 2005 | New CEO of O2 Matthew Key |
| 2005 | YouTube introduced |
| 2006 | Telefonica acquires O2 |
| 2006 | 3G release 99 shortfalls fixed with data technology but needing new investment |
| 2007 | Apple iPhone introduced in 2007 signalling the demise of "the mobile telephone" |
| 2007 | Ofcom retrospectively imposes tighter 3G coverage obligation |
| 2008 | New CEO of Vodafone Vittorio Colao |
| 2009 | First 4G service rolled out but outside of the UK |
| 2010 | WhatsApp first introduced |
| 2010 | Orange merges with T-Mobile to form E |
| 2010 | New CEO of EE Tom Alexander |
| 2010 | Apple's Facetime introduced |

Table 2 - Examples of disruptors to MNO's intended use of spectrum acquired at the 3G spectrum auction

Before the first 3G network was switched on, the Chief Executive Officer of every single winning bidder had changed. There were four more such changes over the subsequent seven years. Three of these were linked to a change of ownership of the mobile network operator. One was linked to shareholder dissatisfaction with the strategy the mobile operator had been pursuing.

In one case, an annual leadership team strategy meeting was held to agree investment priorities. The marketing department put forward a well-researched paper that showed £1m spend on promoting the company's brand with consumers had a significantly bigger impact on the company's share price than £1m spent on improving the 3G network coverage. The company cut back on its next year's investment in the 3G network.

This strategy priority change made perfect sense. Great brands affect consumer emotional buying behaviour. Filling in 3G coverage gaps along country roads does not.

There have also been other major strategy disruptions taking place:

- The emergence of voice over IP technology that undermined telephone call revenues underpinning all the MNOs' auction business cases in 2000.
- The emergence of the Apple iPhone in 2007 that ushered in the era of smartphone that was so instrumental in slicing the integrated mobile services/access market in half between the revenues from the access market that the MNOs monetise and the "over the top" services market revenues that the MNOs cannot.

Finally, there is the practical evidence. Vodafone was the high bidder in the 3G spectrum auction. They were the last to achieve Ofcom's retrospective tighter 3G coverage obligation and did not have a significantly better 3G network than the other MNOs. *In fact, no case has been found that links the highest mobile spectrum bid with the most ambitious network outcome.*

It is reasonable assumption that most bidders (not necessarily all of them as we come to next) will have a business plan that informs their maximum bid. A less safe assumption is that all bidders will not raise their bids beyond the maximum set by their business plans. The least safe assumption is that those business plans won't change, even within a relatively short time after the auction.

*Conclusion: There is a very high probability that the set of assumptions supporting the bidder's ambition on the day of the auction will have changed over the period of an infrastructure business case and certainly over the period of the spectrum licence. Hence, the winning bidders may no longer be pursuing strategies that maximise the economic value of the spectrum.*

### 2.1.2 Auction bids are not always determined by the most productive use

Rational business plans do not always drive the highest bid price. Bids can and have been driven by more strategic aims:

- To shut out further competitive market entry.
- To squeeze the amount of spectrum a competitor can acquire or drive up the price they must pay for it.
- An imperative to acquire a licence at any price. Each generation has been a revolution in the bandwidth of mobile connections. The current allocation they hold is always too narrow to support the new wider bandwidths needed for the next generation of technology. Thus, not acquiring "next generation" spectrum cuts the MNO off from the future – even if they do not have the immediate investment capacity to use the newly acquired spectrum.

*Conclusion: None of these reasons align with the most productive use of the spectrum and while auction design can try to reduce the impact of these strategic aims, it is very difficult to eliminate them. Hence, winning bidders may well not have strategies that maximise economic value to the country.*

### 2.1.3 Substantial mobile network externalities means that there is a lack of alignment of MNOs most productive use (to them) of their spectrum and the most productive use for the country

There was a plausible link in the mobile telephone age between the extent of coverage that was optimal for the MNO to maximise telephone call revenues and the extent that provided the optimal national benefit from a mobile telephone service. However, that link no longer exists in the smartphone age with a mobile broadband network. The massive externality benefits from productivity gains and all the over-the-top services cannot be monetised by the MNOs.

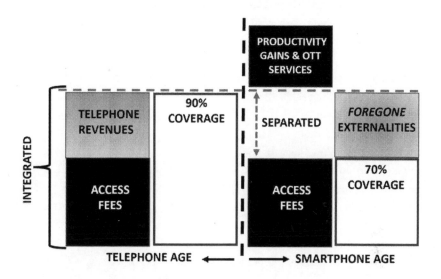

Figure 4 - The separation of the access and "over the top" services market means the extent of coverage in the MNO business case falls short of that had the "externality value" been included

The telephone call revenues have massively shrunk with the popularity of free voice over IP applications. At the same time e-commerce has grown and so has the productivity gains from smartphones. As these substantial externality benefits from all the over-the-top services and productivity gains cannot be monetised by the MNOs, they cannot be reflected in their auction bid prices either.

*Conclusion:   Basing the auction design on the assumption that the most profitable business case for an MNO aligns with the most productive use of spectrum for the country cannot be true for a mobile broadband network with significant externalities, as their value cannot be monetised by the MNO.*

### 2.1.4   Why would a high bidder turn their back on the ambition that would have seen them get their money back with profit?

At the beginning was an idea that underpins the belief that the highest bid price at auctions leads to the highest economic efficiency for the country as, in business, nobody usually invests in an asset without the prospect of that investment paying back with profit in a reasonable time.

This may leave a lingering doubt to settle as to why a high bidder would bid so much money and then be tempted to walk away from an ambition that would have seen them getting their money back with profit.

Not throwing good money after bad as market conditions change provides a compelling commercial answer. Subsequent regulatory actions to lengthen the life of spectrum licences facilitates another. The winning bidder still has the spectrum asset on their balance sheet. Regulators have extended the life of the mobile spectrum licences from an original 10 years to 15 years to 25 years and then to indefinite. Assets are used as collateral to borrow money at lower rates. The spectrum could be traded at any time, perhaps at a profit. In bad times the asset can be written down and the loss set against corporation tax ie reflecting the impairment from not making a return on the spectrum asset. These are all legitimate commercial decisions but none aligning with the economic theory that auctions put spectrum in the hands of the entity making the most productive use of the spectrum for the country.

### 2.1.5  Impact of competition policy on the effectiveness of cash auctions delivering the most economically efficient use of spectrum

There are different competition policy cultures on each side of the Atlantic. The USA competition regulators are more comfortable with market dominance providing that dominance is not abused. Much more prevalent in Europe has been forestalling market dominance. That has been the case in the UK mobile network market.

There has been a conscious effort by Ofcom to sustain a four MNO market, helping the weakest player and limiting the strongest. Evidence of this has been Ofcom imposing regulatory spectrum caps to ensure the strongest does not secure a dominant spectrum holding and advising against mergers. This led to the 2.3 GHz auction that shifted the balance of capacity spectrum holdings.

When each MNO has a portfolio of low and mid band spectrum, where all are using the same global technology standards and all are broadly doing the same things with their spectrum, then the scope for auctions to deliver the most economically efficient use can only be marginal since the economics for all are near-identical.

*Conclusion: The result of competition policy has been to drastically reduce the scope for Ofcom spectrum auctions to deliver any significantly different economic spectrum efficiency outcomes.*

## 2.1.6 Does a link exist between the highest auction bid price and the most economically efficient use of the spectrum for the country?

We said at the outset of this section that there can be three outcomes to our investigation: that a cause-and-effect link can be proved (billions of pounds of economic spectrum efficiency gains visible), or the link is problematic and the gains invisible, or the link appears not to exist at all.

We cannot find a single example where the highest bidder in a spectrum auction has developed a better mobile broadband network than MNOs who left the same auction paying less for their spectrum.

We have brought together a body of evidence and analysis that shows the link is problematic and the gains invisible.

But there are credible doubts the link has ever existed in the UK market.

*Conclusion: It is our opinion that the balance of evidence is that the link between the winning bidders in the auction and the most economically efficient use of spectrum has never existed in the UK market environment.*

This is a liberating conclusion as it frees up Ofcom to be designing future spectrum auctions to meet other policy objectives more demonstrably valuable to the country.

## 2.2    Maximising mobile coverage

Mobile coverage obligations are often attached to spectrum acquired at auction. However, this conflicts with the market approach to spectrum allocation, where the market is supposed to determine "the optimal coverage". But regulators are sometimes pressurized to applying coverage obligations. This is an implicit recognition that auctions will not, without intervention, deliver the most desirable outcome for a country. And with intervention, market forces are not free to deliver as hoped.

As regulators do not require bidders to submit their intended business cases for assessment, they also have no idea at what level to set a coverage obligation. Too severe and no bidders will turn up to the auction. Too lax and they will have not maximised the economic and social benefits to the country. As we show below, they have erred on the side of weak coverage obligations so as not to compromise the market approach.

The 3G coverage obligation at 70% of the population was so weak that Ofcom had to retrospectively impose a tougher one of 90% of the population.

Ofcom was subject to external pressure in imposing a 4G coverage obligation by their Consumer Panel and an early day motion signed by 90 MPs. Ofcom responded by imposing a coverage obligation but only on one of the 800 MHz spectrum packages. Further, they weakened its financial impact by defining a low quality of coverage for enforcement purposes.

There were no coverage obligations on any of the 5G spectrum licences.

*Conclusion: Attaching coverage obligations at spectrum auctions designed following the market approach principles has not been a success in maximising the national economic benefit from new spectrum. The trend has been a move away from them with each new mobile generation.*

## 2.3    Timely way to release new spectrum onto the market

The track record of spectrum auctions getting available spectrum speedily to market is patchy.

The UK was at the leading edge in holding its 3G auction.

The length of time it took the Ofcom to get the 4G spectrum released left the UK trailing other parts of the world by 3-4 years in rolling out its 4G networks. Much of this delay resulted from litigation. That in turn arose from Ofcom interventions over competition concerns. That was a negation of a market approach to spectrum management.

The 5G spectrum auction timing was a mixed result. The first 5G spectrum auction was timely but the industry was left waiting for several years before they could know what their wide radio bandwidths looked like.

The time taken to get out the third of the 5G pioneer bands at 26 GHz has been by far the worst of the delays. The reason given by Ofcom is that they have not seen sufficient demand. But sufficient for what? There has been at least 1 GHz of spectrum just sitting there unused. Other parts of the world already have 26GHz 5G cells deployed to meet intense traffic peaks at locations like international airports and for integrating mobile and front haul applications. The "success" of a market approach design of auction has trumped an early economic benefit from the use of new very high-capacity spectrum.

## 2.4 Effective and transparent means to secure new market entry

Spectrum auctions have been hailed by their advocates as a far superior approach to releasing mobile spectrum than the previous "beauty contest" approach.

### 2.4.1 The myth that spectrum auctions replaced "beauty contests"

There are few UK books or research papers on spectrum auctions that do not repeat the myth that what preceded spectrum auctions were unsatisfactory "beauty contests".

A "beauty contest" was an open international competition run by a government or regulator in which spectrum was awarded to the proposal having the most merit in delivering a national infrastructure goal or augmenting infrastructure competition. The term "beauty contest" arose as companies believed that their chances of getting spectrum might be enhanced by a bidding consortium comprising companies bringing technical competence, financial strength, and some well-respected industrial "brands".

But the impression that this was the way mobile spectrum was awarded before the arrival of auctions obscures the lessons from some of the most successful ways spectrum has leveraged huge infrastructure and economic successes.

Prior to the 3G spectrum auction in 2000 the UK made six awards of mobile spectrum. Three awards went to incumbent mobile operators arising from the duopoly competition policy. One award went to Mercury One-to-One on competition grounds. (Oftel decided this was essential to bolster their fixed wireline challenge to BT[5]). Only two out of six were awarded by a "beauty contest" – the spectrum went to Vodafone and Orange.

The 1G picture is the use of spectrum to pursue the twin objectives of a competition "duopoly policy" and to deliver for the country a high-capacity analogue mobile infrastructure. The first European mobile duopoly emerged in Sweden. The motivation was to widen the opportunity rather than to specifically promote competition. The "duopoly" as a competition measure was pioneered in the UK in 1984 to break the monopoly of British Telecom in the provision of mobile telephone services. The 1G spectrum was split equally. Half went to BT provided they partnered with another company. They chose Securicor. The other half was awarded through an open competition (in the form of a beauty contest) to a consortium of Racal and Millicom. Racal quickly bought out Millicom and spun out a new start up called "Vodafone".

The duopoly policy was a huge success. The sheer competence and competitive spirit of Vodafone galvanised BT/Securicor into an effective response. The competition was fierce right down to the level of public insults flying between CEOs. But it wasn't just hot air being generated. Investments flowed to fuel a race across the UK to be the first to arrive with 1G coverage. It also accelerated

---

[5] See https://www.amazon.co.uk/Casting-Nets-GSM-Digital-TV/dp/1786232618

mobile penetration in the UK. In this way spectrum policy had brought competition and infrastructure policy into alignment.

Prior to 1985, the UK's mobile penetration languished along with that of Germany, France, and Italy in very low single figures.

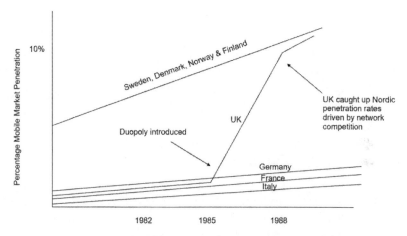

Figure 5– The demonstrable power of the UK duopoly policy

Within three years of the launch of the UK duopoly the UK had five times more customers than that of Germany. In other words, "mobile network competition" had not been the zero-sum game many had feared. The UK's mobile market became the largest in Europe.

The rest of the European Union looked on this brave UK leap into infrastructure competition with a mixture of fear and wonderment at how well it had worked. Fear because nearly all the EU governments were the owners of mobile network monopolies. By 1988 the rest of Europe had drawn their conclusion from the UK network competition experiment. The fixed network competition was judged to have been a failure but the mobile network competition a success. The duopoly competition model was then adopted right across Europe for the new 2G (GSM) technology spectrum release. It was a very significant contributor to the global success Europe had with GSM.

The UK had even more ambitious competition objectives. Just as the rest of Europe was catching up the duopoly, the UK was trail-blazing a four competing mobile network operator market.

Spectrum policy was the critical tool to deliver both the desired competition and quality of infrastructure outcomes. The infrastructure outcome goal was set by the new 1800 MHz networks having to be able to compete effectively with the two already widely deployed national 900 MHz networks. The UK was the first country in the world to deploy spectrum above 1 GHz for cellular mobile. Nobody thought that this feasible as there was known to be a sizable step up of investment needed at 1800 MHz, as far more towers were needed at the high frequency for the same coverage achieved at 900 MHz.

Spectrum and competition policy solutions were fashioned to help the new competitors meet this investment challenge:

- The 1800 MHz operators were given far more spectrum to create more effective competition.
- Spectrum at 38 GHz was given to them to dramatically cut their cost of linking all the extra towers to the core network.
- The 900 MHz operators were required to pay a higher cost for terminating their calls on a new 1800 MHz network than the reverse. Thus the 900 MHz incumbents helped fund the additional cost from the use of a higher spectrum band their competitors had to use.

The spectrum release model that preceding spectrum auctions aligned competition, infrastructure, and spectrum policy to fashion optimal solutions to meet national telecoms policy objectives.

### 2.4.2 "Beauty Contests" as a means for new market entry

For much of the cellular era regulators have been desirous of new market entry. New players it was thought would intensify competition, lower prices, and lead to new services. In "normal" markets new entry does not need to be facilitated – companies observing markets where there appears to be above normal profits, choose to enter in order to share in those profits. This is less the case in cellular. Access to spectrum is a barrier. Not only that, but massive investments are needed in networks and in securing a survivable market share against well-established competitors. History has shown that overcoming this barrier requires regulatory support for a number of years until the new entrant is able to compete effectively and is less vulnerable to aggressively competitive tactics from the well-established players.

We now have forty years of evidence of how well spectrum auctions have been versus "beauty contests" in facilitating successful new market entry. The "beauty contest" approach prevailed over the first period of 20 years with first and second generations of mobile technology. Spectrum auctions have prevailed over the second period of 20 years with third, fourth and fifth generation networks.

Vodafone emerged from the 1G "beauty contest". This start-up grew to become the largest mobile phone operator in the world within a decade. Their mobile infrastructure is extensive and have contributed strongly to UK jobs, research, and international standardisation.

There were two awards made at the 2G "beauty contest" that very quickly consolidated into one. A single company Orange emerged. They created one of the all-time great branding successes with the slogan "the future's bright, the future's Orange". The brand was so strong that when France Telecom came to sell Orange, they kept the name and sold the network and customer base. This emerged as EE and was later acquired by BT.

The branding success was matched by the strength of Orange as a great network engineering company. They managed to create a mobile network at the very challenging 1800 MHz frequencies that provided better coverage in some parts of the country than the two incumbent 900 MHz national networks were achieving. That strength carried into EE and was used to get an early lead in the deployment of 4G networks. Today EE have by far the best mobile network coverage, bolstered with the extra towers resulting from their success in winning the Home Office Emergency Services Network contract.

We now turn to the performance of spectrum auctions.

### 2.4.3 "Spectrum Auctions" as a means of new market entry

As observed above, while in theory a new entrant could just compete in an open auction, in practice they need special treatment to overcome the huge disadvantages of being a late entrant in an established market. This was done through setting aside one of the 3G licences for a new entrant reducing the bidding pressure on that licence and so making it cheaper – another distortion of pure market forces.

No UK spectrum auctions has since set aside spectrum for a new entrant.

The 4G auction saw a BT subsidiary, Niche Spectrum Ventures, successfully win some 2.6 GHz spectrum. The spectrum was never used by BT.

A very innovative enterprise called Dense Air tried to secure spectrum at the first of the 5G auction for a "neutral host" play. They were eliminated very early in the bidding. There were no new entrant bidders at the second 5G auction.

Thus, the only new entrant MNO to come through spectrum auctions is Three, and that only happened by moving away from a pure auction and setting aside spectrum for this purpose. Otherwise, spectrum auctions have proved to be "a hostile environment" for fostering new entrant competitors.

The early efforts of Three were nothing short of heroic. In the first few years they found themselves doing most of the heavy lifting to get 3G off the ground as other UK MNOs were preoccupied in getting their debts down from overpaying for their 3G spectrum.

Three then found themselves on a treadmill of having to cut prices or give bigger bundles just to sustain a survivable market share. They never managed to break out their "disruptor" role.

Based on the evidence "spectrum auctions" have not been more successful than "beauty contests" in securing effective new market entry. But the comparison is not entirely fair as the market conditions were more benign for 1G and 2G than for 3G, 4G and 5G. This leads onto testing a "what if" the new 3G entrant had been selected by a "beauty contest" instead of a spectrum auction?

### 2.4.4  What if the new 3G entrant had been chosen through a beauty contest instead of having to bid at the 3G spectrum auction

The evidence is that only incumbent mobile operators win spectrum at an open spectrum auction. They can outbid every other user and use for the spectrum. As mentioned earlier, the reason is that their huge existing embedded national infrastructure and customer base gives them an unassailable advantage. We suggest[6] that a regulator considering which new entrant in a beauty contest would likely be able to compete most effectively with incumbents would select the one with the greatest existing infrastructure that could be rapidly re-purposed to deliver widespread mobile coverage. The new entrant bidders were:

- MCI Worldcom
- SpectrumCo Ltd (a consortium comprising Sonera Corp., Tesco, EMI Group and Nextel Communications and the Virgin Group)
- Telefonica (the principal Spanish telecommunications operator)
- 3G (UK) Ltd (owned by Ireland's eircom)
- Crescent Wireless (with the same principal shareholders as a new alternative optical fibre telecommunications carrier Global Crossing)
- Epsilon Tele.Com Plc, (a bidding vehicle set up by the Japanese bank Nomura)
- One.Tel Global Wireless Ltd (from Australia)
- TIW UMTS, (a subsidiary of the Canadian enterprise TIW)
- ntl in partnership with France Telecom

There is only one bidder on that list that had any significant existing embedded national infrastructure assets and customer base. That was ntl. They had a national fibre optic network, owned half the TV towers in the UK and many of the Mercury One-2-One towers outside of the M25. They also had a growing telephone customer base from their local cable TV networks and provided the Internet platform for Virgin. Their bid was backed by France Telecom who provided not only huge financial strength but also had one of the finest telecom research labs in the world (CNET). The understanding within ntl was that, had

---

[6] Of course, we can never know for certain what those in a regulator would have concluded, but on rational criteria a significant extent of existing infrastructure provides an unassailable advantage.

the joint venture won the licence, France Telecom would have acquired ntl in its entirety. No other 3G bidder came anywhere close to matching this combination of relevant assets in place and financial strength[7].

So what if ntl had become the UK's fifth mobile network operator via a beauty contest?

If ntl had won, then it is likely that their combination of significant network resources (masts and backhaul) and FT's financial strength would have enabled them to relatively quickly deploy a network of commensurate coverage and capacity to the other MNOs. Vodafone would have had to have disposed of Orange to another buyer. Competition would then have been more on an equal basis, with less need for the maverick approach Three found itself having to resort to. Consumer prices might have been a little higher but overall network coverage and capacity would have been better.

Instead, Three won and has not been particularly successful. They have periodically tried to merge, with O2 and currently with Vodafone and have never managed to get the same level of coverage as the other MNOs. Their maverick tactics (such as allowing free Skype calls before others) certainly shook up the market and may be a contributor to the low margins now experienced by many MNOs.

But that was not the end of the ntl's mobile story. As it happens, they did eventually become one of the UK mobile network operators. Rebranded as Virgin Media, they acquired O2. And a nice twist of fate is that O2 used to be owned by the incumbent BT, who eventually got back into mobile network operations when they acquired "beauty contest" winner Orange (rebranded EE).

This double twist of fate was the reason for including this theoretical exercise, as it allowed us to pose questions about whether, had the country stuck with

---

[7] This raises the question as to why ntl did not win the bid. The answer is due to a complex set of potential merger and acquisition discussions which meant France Telecom had various options open to them and chose to change who they backed, preventing ntl from bidding at the unexpectedly high levels of the auction.

"beauty contests", it would it have finished in a better place with the quality of its mobile networks. The answer is – probably yes.

*Conclusion: Spectrum auctions designed to follow the market approach are not of any use for new market entry purposes. That does not mean we are fans of "beauty contests". They belong to a bygone era.*

## 2.5  Raising the maximum amount of money for the Treasury

### 2.5.1  Everyone wants to know about the money

Whenever the media raise with the Government or Ofcom how much money a spectrum auction raised there is a pained look. The spokesperson patiently explains that the purpose of a spectrum auction is not to raise money. Instead, it is to put the spectrum in the hands of the entity who will make the most productive use of it. But try as they may, the media and public still judge the success of a spectrum auction by how many billions it raises. The answer is summarised in Table 3.

| Spectrum Auction | |
|---|---|
| 3G | £22.5 billion |
| 4G | £2.36 billion |
| 5G (1) | £1.35 billion |
| 5G (2) | £1.36 billion |

Table 3 - How much each spectrum auction raised for the Treasury

The following table shows, in spectrum band order, the unit price of spectrum delivered by the UK 3G, 4G and two 5G auctions:

This table is a story in two halves. The 3G auction is a story in its own right. This is examined in section 2.5.2 below. The other auctions have rational explanations and relevant to future expectations. These are explored in section 2.6.

| Spectrum Band | Unit Price | NOTES |
|---|---|---|
| 700 MHz | £14m/MHz | 5G spectrum auction 2021. Vodafone did not bid. |
| 800 MHz | £22.5m/MHz | 4G spectrum auction 2013 |
| 2.1 GHz | £204.3/MHz | 3G spectrum auction in 2000 |
| 2.4 GHz | £5.1m/MHz | 2018 - O2 the only spectrum winner |
| 2.6 GHz | £5.2m/MHz | 4G spectrum auction in 2013 |
| 3.4 GHz | £7.5m/MHz | 1st 5G auction, so higher price reflects getting a toehold in 5G |
| 3.6 GHz | £4.2m/MHz | 2nd 5G auction saw lower prices as Three did not bid and driver was how wide the 5G radio bandwidth was to be |

Table 4 - Unit price of spectrum as a function of spectrum band

### 2.5.2 The 3G auction exception - it successfully raised loads of money for the Treasury

Was it the Government intention for the 3G auction to raise a lot of money?

The government is a collective of different Ministers and the customary split between politicians and officials. There was certainly a body of view that the primary purpose of the auction was to herald in a new era of managing spectrum based upon market principles. But there is evidence that maximising the money raised for the Treasury was also a shaping force:

1.  There was a widely held view in Government, Oftel and many economists that MNOs were making windfall profits from their spectrum.
2.  The auction prospectus read like a 3G "must buy" sales brochure.
3.  The Treasury forced successful bidders to pay them up front by offering outrageously penal deferred payment terms and then for only half the money.

But none of this explains why the auction spun out of control to such irrational levels. The evidence points to it coming down to the pure chance of its timing.

It was held within just a few weeks of the telecommunication's bubble reaching its very peak. This can be seen in Figure 6 which shows the NASDAQ composite index and Vodafone share price before and after the April 2000 date of the UK 3G spectrum auction. The Vodafone data is a useful indicator as they were a pure mobile player.

Other factors may have been in play, such as sending signals to deter others from entering later 3G auctions held across Europe. But the two highest bidders in the UK 3G auction (Vodafone in the all-comers auction and Three in the new entrant auction) were both linked into the Vodafone/Mannesmann/Orange/France Telecom M&A frenzy.

The Italian 3G spectrum auction was held in October 2000 and only raised around £7.5 billion.

The media poured scorn on the MNO executives for the stupidity of their high bids. But being inside a bubble has a very different criteria of what is rational. The Wall Street Journal best captured the MNO CEO's dilemma. They quoted a Chase Manhattan analyst as saying, "If you fail to get a 3G licence, you're out of the game for ten years." The CEO's had to weigh the soaring bid price of a 3G licence against the stock markets massively hammering their share price the very next day if they came away without a licence.

The conclusion we come to is that the astronomic 3G auction prices were a freak event.

## 2.5.3    The sunk cost question

Economist have argued that the prices paid at auction do not impact the subsequent actions of operators such as the extent to which they deploy a network. They argue that the auction fees are a "sunk cost" and that if large network investment is profitable then this will still occur regardless of the auction fees paid.

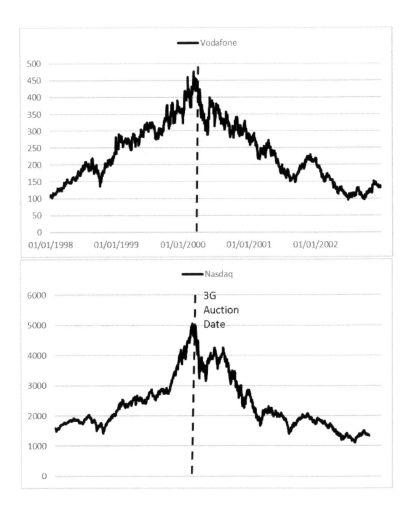

Figure 6 - Pure chance timed the UK 3G auction at the peak of the telecoms bubble

This may be true in respect of MNO's inability to raise prices to recover auction fees. Intense retail competition takes care of that. We do not agree with this in respect of capital investment. While it may be theoretically true, in practice companies are investment constrained. Often, mobile operators will be subsidiaries of international conglomerates (eg as O2 is of Telefonica) where investment is contested between subsidiary companies. Under these conditions what gets spent on spectrum is not available to spend on the network deployment. There is very strong evidence of this after the 3G auction where it is a matter of public record that MNO capital investments right across Europe were slashed. (Anecdotally we are aware of auctions where some operators have pushed up prices knowing their competitors were cash-constrained and seeking to use that to their advantage).

## 2.6 What is really driving the spectrum auction prices

There are three generic drivers determining spectrum auction prices:

1. For covering rural areas, low-frequency spectrum has the range to do this with the least number of towers. Without this spectrum additional towers are needed to deliver equivalent coverage and their cost is high because of the need to bring power and backhaul to a remote site. There can also be long delays in getting planning approval. This makes low band spectrum particularly desirable. There is limited supply, and this makes its price high.

2. For covering urban areas and adding capacity there is already a legacy of a higher density of base stations. This allows the use of high-frequency spectrum for which there is a greater supply. Also, the cost of additional towers is less than that for rural towers. Thus, the value of the higher frequency spectrum is lower.

3. The orchestration of demand for a specific band created by "the next generation" innovation model. The number of determined bidders at any auction has always been what leads to exceptionally high prices. The imperative not to leave an auction empty-handed was a strong factor in the 3G auction. It also explains the price difference between Ofcom's first and second 5G auctions for the 3.4-3.8 GHz band. An MNO had to get spectrum at the first 5G auction just to be in the 5G game. Whereas the second auction was about how wide their radio bandwidth could be.

The above explanations align with the prices shown in Table 4 above. What is coming through is the influence of "infrastructure economics" and "globally standardised next generation technology" cycles on spectrum prices. These factors are common to all the bidders' business cases.

*The conclusion is that bidding for spectrum is far more of a "business cost" of remaining a mobile infrastructure provider than a "market price" of spectrum for some future ambitious venture.*

## 2.7 The Treasury would not lose out if there were no more auctions

From all the above a memo can go to HM Treasury:

- The party is over. The 3G spectrum auction was a freak event. It is never going to happen again.
- "High value" spectrum auctions are for spectrum under 1 GHz. There will not be another one of those coming along for probably 10 years when DTT might (or might not) release some 600 MHz spectrum.
- Meanwhile, all that is in prospect are "capacity bands" higher in the spectrum that don't raise much money at auctions, take a lot of time and effort to organise and provide no spectrum efficiency benefit over just sharing out the spectrum or some exchange of spectrum for infrastructure improvements.

*Conclusion: The most important message of all is that the Treasury will, in future, get far more revenue in the long term from corporate profits, productivity gains and increased economic activity from the substantial externalities a better mobile network infrastructure will deliver than it will from auction fees.*

## 2.8 In summary

This chapter has looked at whether auctions of cellular spectrum have delivered on the following objectives.

1. Making the most economically efficient use of the spectrum.
2. Vehicle to maximise mobile coverage.
3. Timely way to release new spectrum onto the market.
4. Effective and transparent means to secure new market entry.
5. Raising the maximum amount of money for the Treasury.

Taking them in reverse order:

*Raising money for the Treasury* - Whilst the public purpose of cash spectrum auctions is not to raise money, the Treasury has been a significant beneficiary and may thus be reluctant to see the Government seek to change the status quo. The evidence we have presented is that that auction revenues have been on a downward trend for decades and this is likely to continue and even accelerate. This suggests it may be timely for the Treasury to be looking more to the externality benefits from an excellent national set of advanced and more universal essential quality of coverage raising productivity.

*Effective means to secure market entry* – UK spectrum auctions have become a hostile environment for new market entry.

*Timely release of new spectrum* – Timeliness of new spectrum releases has been patchy.

*A means to maximise mobile coverage* – Coverage obligations have not been a conspicuous success. They have not sat well with auctions designed to align with a market approach. In fact, the cash raised may have been having a detrimental impact on the quality of mobile coverage. This is addressed more fully in the next section.

*Making the most economically efficient use of the spectrum* – It is our opinion that the balance of evidence is that a link between the highest auction bid price and the most economic spectrum efficient use for the country has never existed in the UK mobile network market, but if it has existed, the link is tenuous, and its benefits are invisible. Thus there have been no discernible national economic spectrum efficiency gains from auctions designed around the market approach compared with earlier spectrum release approaches, or with auctions that could have been designed with a sole policy objective of improving infrastructure quality. The financial cost to the industry has been huge and, as we will see in the next chapter, the approach has resulted in collateral damage to the quality of a national mobile infrastructure.

# 3 The national infrastructure perspective

The previous chapter has analysed whether spectrum auctions have delivered, or were even capable of delivering, the optimal economic efficiency benefits foreseen in 1999. This section looks from a 2023 perspective, where the spectrum now gets bound into a critical national wireless infrastructure.

As we will come to explain in detail in Part 2, an infrastructure needed to provide a "universal" essential quality of coverage will comprise a zone where the MNOs provide coverage consistent with their access revenues, a zone where there is economic value (from productivity gains and over the top services) that cannot be captured in the MNOs business cases and a third zone where there is little economic case for coverage but may be a societal case. The greatest economic spectrum efficiency in these circumstances comes from the spectrum delivering the high-quality mobile coverage over the first two zones and the greatest societal benefit from an essential quality of coverage over all zones. How successful have spectrum auctions been against this measure?

## 3.1   3G Spectrum Auction

The infrastructure downsides of the 3G spectrum auction are well documented:

- Unprecedented auction prices led MNOs to slash their investments in 3G rollout for several years.
- The supply industry was driven into recession.
- Consumers had a decade of poor 3G mobile coverage.

## 3.2   The 4G Spectrum Auction

This was an auction in two halves. The 800 MHz auction delivered to EE and Three, for the first time, a spectrum band with very favourable range characteristics. This enabled a huge boost in the quality of their coverage. Millions of consumers benefited.

There was also a significant step forward in defining a mobile coverage obligation that was expressed as a percentage of the UK land area and not the traditional but misleading percentage of homes covered. There was anecdotal evidence that this policy emphasis on "geographic coverage" provided a temporary boost to mobile infrastructure competition.

On the downside was the fact that the coverage obligation was watered down to lighten the investment burden.

Whilst the 800 MHz auction could be said to be "a success" that was not the case with the 2.6 GHz auction. It misallocated this potentially valuable "capacity relief" spectrum. There were two contributory factors. The first was that the UK was no longer seen as the best place to invest for a multinational company like Telefonica. They prioritised getting 800 MHz spectrum over the 2.6 GHz spectrum.

The second factor was an unfortunate slip up in the auction rules. The prospective bidders had to separately register for 800 MHz or 2.6 GHz auctions. Our understanding is that Telefonica O2 did not believe they had enough money to bid for both, so they did not register for the 2.6 GHz part of the auction. Much to their surprise they secured their 800 MHz spectrum and had money to spare to bid for some 2.6 GHz spectrum. But the auction rules stopped them from bidding. BT were then able to opportunistically secure some 2.6 GHz spectrum at low cost that they never used.

From the standpoint of auction theory this was the fault of Telefonica, and they would suffer the consequences. But it was not Telefonica shareholders or O2 executives' bonuses that suffered from O2's failure to acquire 2.6 GHz spectrum. It was millions of consumers who suffered. O2 had much higher congestion on their network and as a result consumers had lower data rates or sometimes no useful connection at all.

According to the economic theory, customers should have switched to a different network, but most were unaware that other networks were better due to inadequate consumer information. Ofcom and MNO coverage maps only show basic connectivity and not capacity. Even if such capacity maps had existed, they would be hard for consumers to interpret as users typically pass through many cells that will have different traffic loadings at different times of the day. In other words, there was an inevitable information market failure. As a result, most consumers did not switch. O2 maintained their high market share.

This then became Ofcom's problem. The matter was redressed by a 2.3 GHz spectrum auction[8] where Ofcom, in Command & Control mode, set a cap on BT/EE spectrum holdings that precluded them from bidding. This facilitated Telefonica O2 acquiring their much-needed capacity spectrum.

That Telefonica de-prioritised upgrading the quality of their UK mobile network should have been a loud warning signal - the market in capital is global and the global financial markets were no longer prioritising investment in the UK mobile networks. The pressure was now in the direction of exiting the market.

## 3.3   The 5G Spectrum Auctions

The two 5G spectrum auctions had significant adverse consequences from an infrastructure viewpoint.

### 3.3.1   The loss of the low latency capability of 5G

The promise of the 5G technology was the combination of large capacity and low latency. This offered a visionary future of a tactile Internet of almost limitless bandwidth. There was much fanfare of how 5G would enable this exciting possibility. Then silence from everyone on the 5G's low latency benefit when the 5G networks came to be rolled out.

What happened to *the low latency power* of the new 5G high-capacity networks? The 5G pioneer band of greatest importance has been the 3.4-3.8 GHz band. It had the required capacity and reasonable coverage. But the band also happened to have an incumbent user. It was a small company (UK Broadband) with minuscule coverage but making big claims to aspire to become the UK's fifth mobile operator. They employed a variant of 4G technology with its associated relatively high latency.

---

[8] https://www.ofcom.org.uk/__data/assets/pdf_file/0030/81579/info-memorandum.pdf

UK Broadband's spectrum licence was coming up for renewal at the very same time Europe was designating the 3.4-3.8 GHz band as the sweet spot 5G pioneer band. There was a policy choice. Get UK Broadband to retune their systems to another band (onerous for a small company). Or have the 5G operators fit around the incumbent use. This meant aligning their signal frame structures with the much higher latency of 4G technology in use by the incumbent.

It is not clear that Ofcom ever realised they had this policy choice. Nevertheless, they acted in accordance with the duties put upon them by the 2003 Communications Act. This gave them a principal duty to promote competition. It did not give them a principal duty to improve the quality of the UKs public mobile networks. They renewed the incumbent's spectrum licence.

But the story does not end here. One of the MNOs flagged to the University of Surrey the existence of a low latency option in the global 5G standards. It was called the mini-slot. It would have needed the agreement of all the winners of 5G spectrum. The University of Surrey flagged this in a paper to Ofcom. The Ofcom response was that "this was a matter for the industry". Industry was struggling to sort out the fragmentation resulting from the auction - so it never happened.

Some experts were sceptical of the claims being made for the tactile Internet. Nevertheless, there was a majority expectation[9] at the time that low latency would be important, and auction design and the market approach led to this infrastructure advantage not getting delivered.

### 3.3.2 The 5G spectrum inversion of optimal use

A technically efficient outcome from the 5G auction would have been for the amount of 5G spectrum to broadly match MNO customer market share (spectrum following the customer)[10]. For example, if there are two data pipes,

---

[9] One of the authors was in the minority, see "The 5G Myth" by William Webb

[10] In a true market, there is an argument for allowing unequal outcomes from auctions so that operators can pursue different strategies and the market can allow better ones to win out. But, as explained earlier, with MNOs all using the same technology in the same bands and with regulators preventing one player becoming stronger than the others, there is no real scope for different strategies.

one large and one small and two cohorts of customers, one large and one small, matching the largest cohort of customers to the largest data pipe and the smallest cohort to the smallest pipe gets hugely more economically productive data flowing through than the converse. How efficient were the 5G spectrum auctions against this efficiency measure?

In 2018 the market shares were in the ranking order: BT, O2, Vodafone and H3G. After the 5G spectrum auctions the mobile operators with the most customers finished with the least 5G spectrum and the mobile operator with the least customers finished with the most.

| MNO | Customer share | Mid-band spectrum share |
|---|---|---|
| O2 | 40% | 18% |
| EE | 27% | 18% |
| Vodafone | 19% | 20% |
| Three | 11% | 45% |

Table 5 - The 5G spectrum allocation efficiency failure in numbers

The infrastructure legacy of this will be underused capacity sitting alongside congestion. Congestion depresses demand. It was not economically optimal.

### 3.3.3   A fragmentation mess

It became clear at the first auction that Ofcom leaving the small incumbent user in the band was going to lead to a fragmentation mess. It imposed an overhang on how much spectrum to bid for. To Ofcom's credit they did show flexibility at the second 5G auction to allow bidders to confer before bidding for where their bandwidth would finish in the band. The irony is that the MNO that had paid the most for their spectrum was the one least able to make the most economically efficient use of it - as they were the only one finally caught out with a fragmented 5G bandwidth – leading to both an implementation cost and efficiency loss.

### 3.3.4 Pricing bias against wide RF bandwidths

The auction design led to the most ambitious bidder having a disproportionate impact on the price the less ambitious bidders were forced to pay just to get a toe hold in 5G. Specifically:

- Vodafone trying to secure the most bandwidth got it at a price of £29.7m per MHz.
- This drove-up the cost to BT and O2 to £118m and £125m per MHz respectively to acquiring a minimum wide bandwidth channel.

The resulting spectrum difference was not going to have a material effect compared to sharing out the spectrum equally. That point was not lost on the MNOs when it came to the second of the 5G mid band spectrum auctions where their demands converged. If the goal of the 5G auction design was to deliver the most economically efficient use of the spectrum between the MNOs, the outcome was the opposite.

*Conclusion: 5G auctions designed for the market approach have had a deleterious impact on the on the quality of the UK's national mobile infrastructure.*

## 3.4 Summary of the market approach to spectrum auction design

Where we have come out:

- The links between the highest auction bid price and the most economically efficient use of the spectrum for the country most likely has never existed in the UK mobile network market environment or, if it has, the link has been problematic, and its benefits are invisible.
- The approach has been extremely financially extractive (around £27.5 billion).
- Each of the 3G, 4G and 5G spectrum auctions has had unintended consequences on the quality of the UK's national mobile infrastructure.

This conclusion frees up Ofcom to consider alternative release approaches that may well be less onerous and deliver a far better policy outcome in some circumstances.

If the market approach to spectrum auctions has failed to deliver its economic spectrum efficiency claims, what about the other economic tools of trading and pricing? We turn to these in the next two chapters.

# 4 Spectrum trading vision

The compelling argument in favour of the market approach to spectrum was the claim that "spectrum trading" would lead to a market in spectrum whereby innovators would be able to buy the spectrum they needed when they needed it. No more having to queue up outside the regulator's door. It was a great vision.

| Year | Seller | Buyer | Type |
|------|--------|-------|------|
| 2012 | EE | Hutchison 3G | Public wireless operator |
| 2013 | UK Broadband | Arqiva | Spectrum Access |
| 2013 | MLL | MLL32 | Spectrum Access |
| 2015 | Qualcomm | Vodafone | Spectrum Access |
| 2015 | Qualcomm | Hutchison 3G | Spectrum Access |
| 2016 | Telefonica | Telefonica + Vodafone | Public wireless operator |
| 2016 | Vodafone | Telefonica + Vodafone | Public wireless operator |
| 2019 | Telefonica | Telefonica | Public wireless operator |
| 2019 | EE | Telefonica | Public wireless operator |
| 2019 | Telefonica + Vodafone | Vodafone | Public wireless operator |

Table 6 - Extract from the Ofcom register of trades

It can be seen from Table 6 just how few trades there have been and of these trades most were required as part of the terms of mergers and similar. Since the market in spectrum was so pivotal to driving spectrum economic efficiency gains, it is worth probing to see what happened.

## 4.1 A vision needing scale and scope

The fathers of the market approach to spectrum had an uncompromising belief that the market could do a lot better job of optimising a nation's use of spectrum than governments ever could. Therefore all spectrum should be tradable, and every spectrum use, and user would be subject to the disciplines of the market where the price signals would see spectrum gravitate to its most economically productive use. Governments would pay a market price for spectrum to meet societal needs. Some saw the emergence of spectrum brokers facilitating spectrum trades (and indeed some did emerge but had insufficient income and soon shut down). Some in Ofcom even said that, in the fullness of time, Ofcom would be out of the spectrum management business.

Critical to the success of this vision was "change of use". If the incumbent users of bands that had potential to be used for cellular were able to trade their spectrum to cellular operators, then there would be no need to clear and auction spectrum. Because cellular spectrum is worth much more than any other sort, then there were strong market incentives for this to happen.

But then the real world intruded.

## 4.2 Abandonment of the Coase Theory

The intellectual father behind the market approach to spectrum, Ronald Coase, set out a theory that when property rights were well-defined and transaction costs were low, individuals could bargain and reach efficient outcomes, regardless of the initial allocation of property rights. It did not need the regulator or government to be in the way. He used a land use dispute between two farmers to illustrate how this could work. This is a simplified version of his examples.

Imagine there is a cattle rancher and a farmer living next to each other. The rancher's cattle sometimes stray onto the farmer's land and damage the farmer's crops. The farmer, in response, asks the rancher to either keep the cattle fenced in or to compensate the farmer for the damage caused by the cattle.

Now, there are two possible scenarios to consider:

Scenario 1: The farmer has the property rights to his land. If the farmer has clear property rights and can exclude the cattle from his land, then he can negotiate with the rancher. The rancher may offer to pay the farmer for the right to let his cattle roam, and they could agree on a price.

Scenario 2: The rancher has the property rights to let his cattle roam freely. In this case, the farmer might offer to pay the rancher not to let his cattle onto the farmer's land. The rancher could agree to keep the cattle fenced in for a fee.

The key insight of the Coase Theorem is that, regardless of whether the property rights initially belong to the farmer or the rancher, if transaction costs are low and property rights are well-defined, they can negotiate and arrive at an efficient outcome. This efficient outcome could involve the payment of compensation, changes in behaviour, or the assignment of property rights to the party who values them most.

The Coase Theorem highlights the importance of well-defined property rights and low transaction costs in facilitating negotiations between parties to resolve externalities and reach efficient solutions. Neither of these transpired in the UK's market approach initiative, as discussed below.

### 4.2.1 Property rights

Spectrum has never had a clear property right. While the rights to transmit are relatively clear, the rights to low levels of interference are much vaguer. Apart from a general promise to keep licensed users free from harmful interference there is little to tell a licence holder what they might expect.

Much worse, from the point of view of trading being able to repurpose spectrum usage, almost all licences are use-specific. A cellular licence only allows cellular operation. A broadcast licence only broadcasting. And so on. With this use-case restriction it is completely impossible to trade spectrum from one use to another. It is pointless for a cellular operator to buy broadcasting spectrum when there is no guarantee that the regulator will allow a change of use. *This was a critical flaw in the spectrum trading vision.* Without change of use, trading could only at best shuffle spectrum between competitors in the same use.

Ofcom were aware of this and developed a whole new approach to property rights termed Spectrum Usage Rights (SURs)[11]. These were radically different

---

[11] https://www.ofcom.org.uk/__data/assets/pdf_file/0023/36527/final_report.pdf.

from current licences. Rather than restrict the maximum power that could be transmitted, they restricted the maximum interference that could be caused. Because the key risk of a change of use was that interference could rise, Spectrum Usage Rights overcame this risk and so were inherently technologically neutral. A Spectrum Usage Right licence did not need to state what it could be used for. Even better, by looking at the Spectrum Usage Right licences of spectrum neighbours, it was easy to get a clear understanding of the interference level that could be caused. It was a fully defined property right that would allow, for example, a cellular operator to buy broadcast spectrum and repurpose it. Spectrum Usage Rights were critical to the vision of trading.

Ofcom went as far as to award a licence in the Spectrum Usage Right format – the "L-Band" licence auctioned in 2005 which was won by Qualcomm. Interestingly, it was bought for mobile TV broadcasting (an application that did not subsequently emerge), Qualcomm got the global mobile standard's body to embrace the band (increasing its value) and then traded it to Vodafone for cellular usage. This is exactly what trading could have achieved – change of use, value enhancement and purchase by mobile operators of non-cellular spectrum.

After its success with L-Band, Ofcom planned to apply Spectrum Usage Rights to the forthcoming 4G auction. But there was strong push-back from the MNOs. They felt that Spectrum Usage Rights were untried, and therefore risky, and that this could make it harder to value 4G spectrum. They were also concerned about the increased complexity of their verification. The success of the 4G auction was judged potentially to be at risk and the benefits of Spectrum Usage Rights insufficient to take such a risk. The 4G licences were issued using conventional transmitter-based restrictions and Spectrum Usage Rights were quietly shelved.

And that was the end of an initiative that might have allowed trading to work and would also have overcome concerns about receiver performance and many other spectrum management challenges.

Were Spectrum Usage Rights widely applied it might have been the case that trading might have delivered on its promise. With the decision not to use them trading could never deliver its promise.

## 4.2.2   Transaction costs

While it might have been relatively low cost for a mobile operator to do a deal with another spectrum user, the resulting regulatory attention would have been anything but cheap and quick. The amount of spectrum each mobile operator owns is carefully tracked and managed by the regulator who are concerned that if one operator gains a significant advantage in spectrum holdings then they will be able to force out their competitors from the market. It is why there are invariably caps in auctions and, when mergers are allowed, why there is usually a requirement to divest spectrum. While it may be an example of a regulator, perhaps incorrectly, distorting a market, it is nevertheless a fact of life for mobile operators.

If an operator were able to acquire non mobile spectrum and re-purpose it (which was not possible after Spectrum Usage Rights were set aside) then the regulator would likely intervene. Dealing with the regulator would probably result in significant legal fees. Even worse, the regulator might then count the spectrum against any future cap, limiting the ability to buy auctioned spectrum which might be better (for example, because more handsets might be able to access it). The costs of such a cap could be disproportionate.

A larger operator buying spectrum from a struggling smaller operator – which would have been possible even without property rights – would almost certainly have been blocked by the regulator, or at least heavily scrutinised.

While transaction costs may have appeared low, the "downstream" costs and delays associated with the inevitable, if misjudged, regulatory intervention could be very high.

## 4.2.3   Economic rationality

Mobile operators and broadcasters may have acted rationally and sold any unused or underused spectrum to redeploy the capital more productively had they the confidence that, when a need arose, there was a high likelihood of buying more. But nobody in the industry believed a market in spectrum would ever emerge. As spectrum is the lifeblood of a wireless business spectrum holders tenaciously cling on to what they had. The absence of a market then became self-fulfilling.

### 4.2.4 While Coase may have been right regulators lacked the will to deliver on his caveats

The Coase theory was compelling. But trading only had value if it could be accompanied by change of use which would allow non-cellular spectrum to be sold to mobile operators who could then repurpose it. This had an absolute requirement - property rights that enabled change of use. Regulators failed to deliver these.

Instead, the regulator continued to clear and auction, feeding the operators all the spectrum they needed through this route. While auctions were expensive to the operator, it was much more certain for them. They could leave the identification of spectrum and its global harmonisation to a willing regulator. Effectively it helped de-risk the sector for the existing MNOs. The high cost of auctioned spectrum shut everybody with other applications out of the market. Regulators were forced to partition off other spectrum for innovators on a first come first served basis at a price just to cover administrative cost.

Put simply, Coase said that it does not matter who has the licences initially, as long as the property rights are well defined, and trading can happen then they will end up in the optimal place. What spectrum regulators around the world have done is the exact opposite. They have gone to great efforts on the original assignment of licences via complex auctions but then failed to define the property rights sufficiently to enable trading. Unsurprising, then, that the hoped-for revolution in spectrum management from market forces failed to happen.

## 4.3 Could a market in spectrum ever have worked

Regulators and politicians talked the talk on the big potential economic gains that spectrum trading would deliver in a market approach. But neither they nor their successors walked the walk. The spectrum auction band waggon rolled on. The political risk was too high of mobile operators hoovering up all the usable spectrum and leaving innovators and many others with nothing. Confidence was also so lacking in the industry such that everyone held on to what they had as the risk that they would not be able to re-acquire spectrum traded away and subsequently needed was too great.

The "market in spectrum" was a radically different approach that left no room for government/regulator to be half in and half out. Either "the market" could be trusted to make more economically efficient use of spectrum resources, or it is not.

## 4.4   Is there any role for spectrum trading?

*Conclusion: There is no reason to stop trading. But it has been relegated to the minor league of economic spectrum efficiency tools. And that implies that its scope for economic spectrum management is very limited.*

In the next chapter we look at the final economic tool – spectrum pricing.

# 5 Mobile spectrum pricing – the ugly sister

## 5.1 Why price spectrum?

The Coase theory says nothing about adding a price to spectrum. Indeed, its recommendation that transaction fees are low and property rights well defined would suggest not adding an annual levy as this complicates any understanding of the future value – since the fees can rise – and by extracting some of the value in any trade, makes a trade less likely.

Pricing was originally applied more as a transition measure. There were two policy objectives, quite different, where it was thought pricing was useful and appropriate:

1.  To encourage those hoarding spectrum to return it to the regulator, since they would now have to pay to hoard. This was only needed until trading was allowed since once spectrum is tradable there is an economic incentive to sell unwanted spectrum.
2.  To provide a measure of "fairness" when auctioning was introduced by charging those who gained spectrum "for free" before the introduction of auctions so that, after a period of time, they would have paid about the same as their competitor who had acquired all their spectrum at an auction.

As we will see, with regards to mobile networks, there was an attempt to use one pricing mechanism to achieve both, and no sunset clauses or similar to acknowledge that they were transitory. Whatever the case for it, an entirely inappropriate pricing scheme emerged.

## 5.2 Discouraging hoarding

Pricing was the very first economic tool introduced in the UK. This happened because the regulator, then the Radiocommunications Agency (RA) had the powers to price spectrum, whereas it did not have the powers to allow trading or auctions. Hence, pricing could be applied immediately, and then removed once trading was enabled.

The idea behind pricing was to face the current holders of spectrum with the cost differential that an alternative use would incur without this spectrum. For example, an alternative user might have to lay fibre optic cable rather than use microwave backhaul or use higher frequency links with multiple hops rather than a single hop. That alternative user would, in theory, be willing to pay this differential for the spectrum because it was worth that much to them. If the current user was willing to pay this differential because they valued the spectrum more than it was appropriate that they should keep it. But if they valued it less than an alternative user, they should return it to the regulator so it could be reassigned (in the absence of trading, the regulator effectively made the trade).

In essence, the regulator was trying to calculate the market price for spectrum had there been a market and then apply this as an annual fee spread across a reasonable amortisation period. So, for example, the cost of a fibre cable might be spread across 20 years and so the annual fee would be $1/20^{th}$ of the cost of the cable.

As can be imagined, this was challenging. Even knowing what the highest value alternative use might be was hard. In the case of cellular, there is no higher value use (something we return to below). Then determining the cost of that alternative use requires many assumptions. Finally, costs can change rapidly as technology improves, suggesting pricing might need to be modified annually.

This led the economists to observe that any calculated price was uncertain. If the price was set too high, they argued, spectrum would be returned but nobody would then apply for it because it was uneconomic to use, so it would remain idle. If it was set too low, then users would not return spectrum because it remained worthwhile to hoard it.

Prices were duly calculated. But then, as always, politics intervened. To soften the blow of a sudden introduction of pricing the decision was made to cut the prices in half. There was no economic justification for this. The result, obviously, was that prices were too low to encourage any return of spectrum. Predictably, pricing then failed to deliver any noticeable return of spectrum.

Subsequently spectrum trading was introduced that gave a larger incentive for MNOs not to hoard spectrum. Spectrum pricing was then no longer needed to meet this policy objective. Trading of radio spectrum licences has been possible since late 2004 and governed later by the Wireless Telegraphy (Mobile Spectrum Trading) Regulations 2011. Therefore, the need for pricing as a market incentive for MNOs not to hoard their spectrum ceased in 2011. This broadly maps to the period of massively rising data demand acting to pull into use all of the mobile operators' spectrum in any case.

### 5.3   Providing fairness

The "level playing field" justification was a fairness argument. However well intentioned, this was without merit for two reasons:

- All the bidders for the first auction – for 3G spectrum - had an HMG auction prospectus that spelt out what was on offer in detail. All the bidders knew who the incumbents were, what they had by way of spectrum, the fact they got it free and what was on offer at the 3G auction. So did Three. Everyone entered the auction knowing what the deal was.
- From the perspective of the incumbent MNOs, there was nothing in the auction perspective that indicated that there was a "level playing field" issue still to be settled.

In the auction, the new entrant (which subsequently became Three) paid £4.4bn for the same amount of spectrum as Vodafone who paid £5.9bn. Three were effectively "gifted" £1.5bn through the auction structure which reserved a licence for a new entrant, compensating them for the challenges of competing with incumbents. This, then, was their recompense for the "free" spectrum that their competitors had been assigned in the past. No further pricing or similar was needed, nor expected.

Even more questionable in terms of fairness was that it was the same Treasury that had agreed the auction prospectus (that set out the terms of the deal), collected the £22.5 billion for the 3G spectrum and subsequently instructed Ofcom to double the annual licence fee to the full opportunity cost.

### 5.3.1 Where were the sunset clauses?

The point has already been made that the justification for the pricing incentive not to hoard spectrum should have lapsed once spectrum trading had been enabled. But the annual fee to level the playing field should also have lapsed once the playing field had been levelled financially.

Of course, none of this happened. There was no end date to the fees, and they rose with inflation and were periodically recalculated.

| | 900MHz | | 1800MHz | | 2100MHz | | Total |
|---|---|---|---|---|---|---|---|
| Operator | MHz | Fee £m | MHz | Fee £m | MHz | Fee £m | £m |
| EE | 0 | 0 | 90 | 79 | 40 | 23 | 102 |
| Vodafone | 34.8 | 41 | 11.6 | 10 | 29.6 | 17 | 68 |
| Telefonica | 34.8 | 41 | 11.6 | 10 | 20 | 12 | 63 |

Table 7 – Annual Licence Fees in 2023 (estimate) with a total, including that from Three, of around £300m

The numbers are only the estimates made by one MNO as annual licence fees for each MNO are not published. But it would be a reasonable guess from these orders of numbers that the playing field had been levelled many years ago relative to the original Ofcom "fairness" policy intention.

If we assumed that these numbers were correct in valuing spectrum, then this would suggest that over 20 years an MNO would pay £1.5bn on average. As shown above, this was the saving that Three gained in the 3G auction, reinforcing the message that fairness had already been delivered at that point.

## 5.4 Spectrum pricing and economic efficiency

Spectrum pricing of mobile operators then continued beyond its natural sunset dates and without any regulatory justification apparent to the industry. Even as a tax it had not been approved by Parliament. So, much to the frustration of the

MNOs, Ofcom's consultation on their spectrum strategy for the 2020's claimed that spectrum pricing had become an additional tool used to create incentives for spectrum to be used efficiently.

Now there are different forms of spectrum pricing. For example, there is one version that can be used to temper demand and there are circumstances where that can make sense. The form of spectrum pricing relevant to Ofcom's market approach is as an incentive for MNO spectrum (not acquired at an auction) to be used more efficiently.

This argument for retaining spectrum pricing for mobile operators was reviewed by an independent study[12] carried out by Analysys Mason in 2022. On their study team was no less than the economist giant in these matters – Prof Martin Cave. Their report concluded that it was no longer needed on spectrum efficiency grounds. Trading already provided sufficient incentives.

But the review did not comment on whether this form of incentive spectrum pricing was a credible tool for having any impact on spectrum efficiency. . Below we look at various explanations we know of as to how it is alleged to work:

1.  Spectrum pricing creates an awareness within MNOs of its value and that awareness leads them to make more efficient use. Global standards bodies determine the technology choices that fundamentally impact how efficiently spectrum is used. They have no idea what prices Ofcom charge for spectrum (nor care). Then, it is the inexorable rise in customer demand for data that determines when and where all of the spectrum gets deployed. Thus, there is no place over the entire process of exploiting the spectrum where "price awareness" leads to anything being done differently.

2.  A more valuable non-MNO use may emerge in the future and keeping spectrum pricing in place would incentivise the MNO to sell the spectrum to this user. The rhetoric question is more valuable use to

---

[12] https://www.analysysmason.com/about-us/news/newsletter/spectrum-market-mechanisms-quarterly/

whom – the purchasing enterprise or the country? This question exposes the flaw, it only compares the value to the MNO and the value to the new non-MNO purchaser. What is missing in the equation is that the MNO use now has externalities of immense value to the country and its use is inextricably tied into a critical national infrastructure.

3.  It incentivises MNOs to sell on any unused spectrum. The pricing incentive has been wrongly defined for this purpose. The price is a nationally defined figure that does not differentiate between areas where the spectrum is fully deployed and areas where spectrum lies unused for years. It therefore cannot incentivise trades for this unused "local" spectrum. Even if the regulations were to be changed to permit trading of local unused spectrum there remains a practical barrier. The value of local spectrum will be related to the local population density. This leads to a ratio of over 1300:1 in local values between the most densely populated areas and the least. The value of spectrum in least populated areas would not cover the legal costs of a trade and the value in the highest density areas is irrelevant as the spectrum is fully used.

4.  There are economic spectrum efficiency differences between MNOs and spectrum pricing provides an incentive for the less efficient MNO to sell spectrum to the more efficient MNO. As all MNOs use the same standardised technology and are connected to the same global Internet providing the same range of services, the spectrum efficiency differences between MNOs are marginal. However, even if there were large spectrum efficiency differences, the idea of the most efficient MNO buying out the spectrum from the less efficient MNO would diminish competition in the market. Anything meaningful would get blocked on competition grounds.

None of these explanations of how administrative incentive pricing delivers or could deliver spectrum efficiency for mobile spectrum are plausible.

## 5.5   A summary of pricing

Pricing should have been a transitory tool, used as markets were becoming established and then removed. Instead, it became a permanent feature, likely inhibiting economic gains. There is no evidence that it has or could incentivise more efficient use of the mobile spectrum in use today, although very different versions of pricing may have roles in other areas. The title of the book "Emperor Ofcom's new clothes" fairly fits what has been happening (or not happening) to this ill conceived form of spectrum pricing these last ten years.

*Conclusion: The claimed spectrum efficiency benefits of mobile spectrum annual licence fees have been as invisible as the emperor's new clothes.*

# 6 A mobile world turned upside-down

If the market approach to spectrum turns out to have failed, it is useful to know if the economic theories were wrong in the first place or whether they may have been right for the world of 1999 but wrong for the world of 2024.

## 6.1 The world of the early to mid-90s

In November 1999 the UK government published a seminal White Paper entitled "Radio Spectrum for the 21st Century: Proposals for the Modernisation of the Use of the Radio Spectrum in the UK"[13].

Viewed from the perspective of 1999 this new market approach to spectrum policy appeared a perfect match to meeting the prevailing challenges that had emerged in the early to mid-1990's. This view is summarised in Table 8.

| |
|---|
| An explosion of wireless innovation leading to a plethora of technology posibilities: many cellular variants, telepoint, short range radio, trunked private radio, two-way paging, LEO satellites and dedicated data systems. |
| Cellular mobile populised amoung the rich and stock market "yuppies". |
| Populisation of the short message service (SMS) delivering high profits from small data transmissions to supplement profitable call revenues. |
| Emergence of walled gardens on the Internet and the prospect of e-commerce. |
| High profit margins for mobile operators. |
| International growth and consolidation. |
| Availability of new spectrum for national networks. |
| Seemingly unlimited financial capital. |

Table 8 - The scene spectrum regulators faced in the early to mid-1990s

---

[13] No longer available on-line.

## 6.2   A mobile world turned upside down in just two decades

Everything was to change over the next two decades. This can be conveniently grouped into three profound changes on the purpose and impact of mobile spectrum policy:

- The "Next Generation" model for cellular mobile innovation.
- The death of the mobile "licence to print money".
- Transition of mobile from a nice-to-have to an essential part of modern economic and social life.

### 6.2.1   The "Next Generation" model for cellular mobile innovation

In May 1987 the Ministers from the four large EU countries (France, Germany, Italy, and the UK) met in Bonn and agreed to come behind a single cellular mobile standard that came to be known as GSM. This decision was implemented in a GSM Memorandum of Understanding. It was initially signed by 13 mobile network operators (MNOs) from 12 countries and very shortly by every MNO in Europe and then many from outside.

The alignment of all the customers (MNOs) for new digital mobile networks created a massive procurement power. It forced all the large system suppliers behind the same technology. They in turn aligned the equipment suppliers they bought from. They in turn aligned the chip vendors. All the mobile handset suppliers had to follow for their products to work with the new networks. The result was a formidable economic engine driving towards almost immediate scale economies.

Every major telecom research lab in the world put their largest resources behind GSM development. The pace of GSM innovation outran that of all the rival cellular mobile technologies. The rise in the scale economies behind GSM also outran all its rivals.

By 2000 all bets were off for rival technologies. Paging all but disappeared along with telepoint, short range radio, private trunked mobile systems, dedicated data system and the various LEO/MEO mobile satellite systems of the time.

Soon all rival cellular mobile standards disappeared. The mid 90's saw many the installed rival systems being ripped out in many parts of the world and replaced by GSM systems or prematurely closed to be replaced by totally standardised "next generation" 3G technology.

Intel led the last significant initiative to take on this giant global mobile innovation monolith with its WiMax technology. It proved a failure.

There ceased to be any task for spectrum market mechanisms to do in sorting out the most profitable or more spectrally efficient mobile technology innovations.

## 6.2.2    Death of the MNO licence to print money

The cellular mobile "licence to print money" fell victim to four irresistible economic forces:

1.    Regulatory attrition.
2.    Fracturing of the mobile services and access markets.
3.    Steeply rising costs of higher capacity national mobile networks.
4.    Attack from "big tech" on both sides of the MNO balance sheet.

Each of these is explained below.

a) Regulatory attrition

The first decade of cellular mobile saw a steep growth in mobile penetration. This rapidly expanding market was highly profitable. Regulators were concerned that a regulatory duopoly was having no effect in bringing prices down. In the UK the two-player market became a four-player market but still prices remained relatively high and profit margins substantial. In 2000 a fifth MNO was introduced.

This broadly coincided with mobile penetration reaching its limit. The new entrant found itself on a treadmill of cutting prices just to hold onto a survivable market share. The other MNOs cut prices to keep them there. This saw prices fall and fall. Competition was finally working to lower prices, but it worked too well and by 2013 was eating into the investment seed corn for future network upgrades.

In addition to competition effects were regulatory actions to lower prices:

- Call termination changes to phone a landline number were eliminated.
- Roaming charges across the EU were eliminated.

Both had an adverse impact on MNO revenues which in turn affected their capacity to attract capital to invest. Competition reduced margins and spectrum auctions and spectrum pricing were financially extractive.

b) Fracturing of the mobile services and access markets

The first MNO new service market opportunity to fall after the 3G auction was the walled garden[14]. No matter how hard MNOs tried to make their walled gardens attractive, consumers found the vast world of Internet content far more compelling. Vodafone poured hundreds of millions into their Vodafone Live! They had a large office in the Strand full of content executives signing deals with content owners. But however fast they ran, the content providers on the wider Internet ran faster. One day a Vodafone executive signed a deal to allow Google onto Vodafone supplied mobiles. This allowed consumers to break out of the walled garden and find the contents they wanted elsewhere. Aghast managers across the company rounded on the poor employee for this treachery who stood their ground and said, "but that is what our customers want". They were right. The walled gardens were dead.

c) Steeply rising costs of national networks working in ever high spectrum bands

MNOs have found themselves on a path of having to provide ever more data capacity to their customers just to hold up access subscription revenues at current levels. But the cost path is a steeply rising one. The reason for this is that providing ever more data requires wider radio bandwidths. This in turn means

---

[14] A walled garden is a subset of the Internet which has been curated to work well on mobile devices and aligns with the MNOs' interests.

using ever-higher bands in the spectrum that have the space. But the higher bands have shorter transmission ranges. Therefore, to cover the same area demands ever-more towers. With capital intensity remaining flat the result has been limited coverage at the higher frequency bands.

d) Attack from "big tech" on both sides of the MNO balance sheet

The single biggest source of MNO revenue and profit over the first decade of mobile network operations was telephone and SMS call revenues. Both have been whittled away by comparable services provided by Internet "big tech" companies "free of charge". In the case of WhatsApp, the video telephone is thrown in as part of the proposition. No matter how efficient an MNO is, there is no way to compete profitably with something given away free.

On the cost side has been the explosion of video from YouTube, Netflix, and others. This has created a mobile business model where the MNOs have no control on the demand side of their businesses. Net neutrality regulation precludes using price to manage demand. Intensity of retail competition effectively blocks the MNOs from passing more than a fraction of the rising costs onto their customers.

## 6.2.3  Transition of mobile from "a nice -to-have" to an essential part of modern economic and social life

The first mobile telephones cost £2,000 (£6,000 in today's money). It was a nice -to-have luxury. One can draw a line from 1985 (when the first hand portable mobile phone arrived in the UK) to around 2005 when the mobile first broke through "the less than $30" barrier. Rising in the other direction has been the penetration numbers reaching near 100%. Everyone had a mobile.

The iPhone first emerged in 2007 and began the market transition from the mobile telephone to the smartphone. The penetration curve rose even faster and by 2012 the smartphone had become dominant.

Somewhere on that journey (probably around 2013) the mobile network had transitioned from "a nice-to-have" private sector venture that could be left to the market to an indispensable national infrastructure that could not. This brought with it new cost burdens on the MNOs to ensure the security and resilience of their networks, for example, the high-risk vendor regulation[15].

The net result has been that the MNOs needed to minimise investment in network upgrades to stay financially viable.

## 6.3   The World Today

This brings us to today, where things could not be more different than the view from 1999. Table 9 summarises this quite different world:

| |
|---|
| Mobile networks become a part of the critical national infrastructure. |
| All MNOs provide the same service (mobile Internet access) using the same globally standardised technology and in many cases sharing the same masts. |
| Little or no international demand to enter the UK mobile network market. |
| Little mobile network competition but intense retail competition. |
| Falling expectation that MNOs will deliver improved coverage and a USO. |
| MNOs business models weak with some appearing to have returns below the cost of capital. |

Table 9 - The scene spectrum regulators face today that began to crystalise around 2013

The table below shows the key objectives for regulators around the time market mechanisms were given serious consideration and now.

| Key regulatory objectives in 1999 | Key regulatory objectives in 2023 |
|---|---|
| • Inject increased competition into the cellular market. | • Improve the essential quality of universal mobile coverage. |
| • Officials giving way to markets to make optimal use of spectrum. | • Overcome the infrastructure investments deficit. |
| • Markets deciding between the plethora of technology choices. | • Improve UK network resilience, security, and open procurement. |

Table 10 – Comparison of key regulatory objectives

---

[15] This has required MNOs to remove equipment sold by Huawei and other Chinese vendors from their networks.

The 1999 objectives read like ones that a market might be expected to deliver. Competition and innovation are features of a vibrant market and trading might have been expected to free up spectrum for innovators. Less so the 2013 and 2023 objectives.

For some time, telecommunications infrastructure has no longer been attracting the levels of investment needed from the international financial markets. Consumers do not want to pay more. The state of the public finances precludes significant public subsidy. The MNOs capacity to step up investment has become overly depleted. There is little interest to enter the UK mobile market. Against this background the 2023 objectives read more like objectives that require significant intervention.

## 6.4 The theories might have been right in 1999 but are wrong now

Did Ofcom get it wrong shortly after its foundation in 2003 when it set out a strategy of relying increasingly on markets?

It could be argued that the issues listed in the first part of this book could have been foreseen. Trading would fail because establishing a market in spectrum would be too difficult and because spectrum could be used as a tool to prevent competition and to entrench advantaged positions. Auctions would not deliver optimal outcomes because of "behavioural economics", irrational beliefs from stock markets and shareholders and the difficulty in predicting the future resulting in frequent changes of direction.

But this would be too much of a hindsight view. In 1999 it was far from clear to policy makers what the optimal use of mobile spectrum looked like. There were far too many emerging mobile technology choices for each to have its own spectrum (that was the demand at the time) and too many chances of making the wrong decisions. Future market dynamics were unknown and the case for a market approach was rational given the challenges at the time and the wide consensus that either supported it or suspended judgement and was willing to give it a go.

We have charted what happened. Auctions have no impact on how well spectrum is used, trading does not happen because of poor definition of rights, and pricing does not help because it is used in the wrong places. There is less need for markets to determine optimal outcomes in a world where all use the same technology to deliver the same services, with very little scope for innovation or differentiation. Markets rarely deliver socially desirable outcomes, and these have become ever more important as mobile networks have become part of the critical national infrastructure.

The failure of the market approach to spectrum to deliver against an aspiration of markets moving spectrum to the most efficient use can be put down to two very different reasons at two different time.

1. At the start was a failure of political nerve to embrace the market approach across the piece and do whatever it took for it to succeed. A parallel can be drawn to leaping over a wide river from one bank to the other. It is never a good idea to leave one foot on the departing side[16]. This left a half-hearted market approach to spectrum wrapped around just one industry.
2. The second reason was that the market, industry, and regulatory framework became the victim of massive global forces that turned the industry up-side-down.

Ofcom's position set out in their spectrum management strategy for the 2020s is "Relying on market mechanisms where possible and using regulatory levers where necessary".

*Conclusion: This examination has shown that Ofcom's efforts to hold onto the "belief" in the market mechanisms only continues a 21ˢᵗ Century version of the fable of the emperor's new clothes. Its economic spectrum efficiency benefits are invisible. Time and effort will be more productively spent for consumers, citizens, and the country on making a success of the next revolution and not*

---

[16] In this case, the "foot that remained" was Ofcom's continuation of clearance of new spectrum for mobile (a command & control activity) rather than requiring the market to repurpose the spectrum itself.

*being distracted chasing invisible benefits from the remnants of the last failed revolution.*

# 7 What could have been done differently?

As discussed in the previous chapter, introducing the market approach to spectrum as early as 1999 was a bold initiative well matched to the challenges at the time. We do not suggest any different course open at the time offered an obviously better way to manage spectrum. But as this book has shown, market forces have not worked as hoped and now appear ill-suited to delivering the needs of the UK for world-class mobile connectivity. Where did it go wrong, and what action should have been taken as soon as this had become evident?

## 7.1 Early alarm bells

As noted in Chapter 4 for market forces to work, well defined property rights that allowed change of use were essential. The failure to implement these for the 4G auction should have prompted a serious review of whether Ofcom, and the UK Government, were still fully committed to market forces, with all that implied.

## 7.2 Becoming utilities – the turning point

The most visible turning point was when operators had become utilities. By this we mean the point when the consumer offering from MNOs was indistinguishable and interchangeable. This was reached when MNOs were fully committed to the same global standards, connecting to the same Internet, and stopped believing that they could develop innovative new mass market services of their own.

Utilities require a very different kind of regulation from rapidly growing enterprises in rapidly changing innovation-driven markets. The former needs interventionist policies designed to promptly address market failures, prevent monopoly behaviours and to deliver socially desirable outcomes. The latter needs a light touch and unfettered market guidance.

The change from an innovative growth market to a utility market did not happen overnight, but the alarm bells should have been ringing with policy makers around 2014. By then the shape of the huge emerging transformational changes listed in the previous chapter were becoming clearer. Instead, there has been almost a lost decade in which some MNOs made strenuous efforts to find a high growth story and the regulator kept them in a financially extractive spectrum framework as if they had.

## 7.3  What good would have looked like

A better outcome for the UK in 2023 would have been:

1.  Ubiquitous basic coverage across close to 100% of the country and in trains, buildings and elsewhere.
2.  Integrated cellular/Wi-Fi networks that provided excellent indoor coverage and capacity.
3.  Sufficient broadband network capabilities for all mainstream applications – often taken to mean widespread 5G deployment, although 4G may be sufficient in many areas.
4.  Network procurement that promoted UK skills and rising investment in research.

There are various ways this might have been achieved, and it is worth reflecting that for most utilities there is a single pipe or wire (eg gas, water, electricity) but then competition at the retail level. As mobile networks have become more utility-like their delivery could have become more like a single network, but Ofcom, with the exception of mast sharing and the shared rural network (SRN), has resisted MNO consolidation that may have weakened retail competition.

## 7.4  Doing things differently

Currently the Government's infrastructure ambition is made known to an independent regulator through a non-binding strategic statement. On the other side of the divide come spectrum auctions when Ofcom judge the demand is there. Auction outcomes are a market process and therefore unpredictable. Sometimes the outcomes will be helpful, sometimes they pull in the opposite direction and sometimes neither one nor the other. This highly inefficient approach to the periodic modernisation of a critical national infrastructure arises because Ofcom:

- Was never given by Parliament a principal duty to design their auctions to deliver the Government's national infrastructure goals.
- Follows a quite different policy objective for their auction design based on economic theories (since overtaken by events).

A different approach would have seen a much greater policy alignment between the government's industrial and societal objectives for improving national wireless infrastructure and Ofcom's mobile spectrum policy. The Government poses the problems and Ofcom is then left to find the best solutions. Had this happened in 2014 we might have seen, for example, a very different approach to 5G spectrum with a clean mid band and with licences being traded for coverage, capacity, and network supply obligations[17] to a mutually agreed timeline. It might have sent stronger signal much earlier to MNOs that the right sort of consolidation was acceptable and planned and delivered a much more extensive Shared Rural Network much sooner.

What has happened is the UK finds it mobile spectrum policy caught between two worlds. Spectrum auctions and spectrum pricing are still semi-attached to the 1999 world and a failed market approach philosophy. A market approach being applied in a circumstance where there is no market cannot deliver expected benefit and its effect on the national mobile infrastructure can only be haphazard. Therefore, what is being delivered in 2023 is a sub-standard mobile network infrastructure and sub-optimal economic spectrum efficiency.

---

[17] We note that enforcing network supply obligations such as coverage obligations has historically proven very difficult. Determining coverage is hard, and imposing fines on companies may diminish their ability to meet obligations. Clearly, if a new approach relies on obligations, then better mechanisms to measure and enforce them will be needed. Techniques such as contracts that pay the MNOs only on the completion of milestones or similar may be needed. This is for further study.

## 7.5 In summary – generally the right decisions at the time by well-meaning players

A retrospective judgement must take account of what the prevalent problem was facing spectrum regulators at the time. It is our conclusion that the decision to go for a market approach made sense, given that hitherto efforts to find new spectrum for every new emerging technology was not sustainable when so many rival mobile technologies were all emerging at the same time. Our retrospective criticism is directed at the lack of willingness to do it with a level of commitment that might have delivered success.

The market vision was predicted on the Coase Theorem that said that the initial distribution of licences was unimportant because as long as property rights were well defined and trading unimpeded, then the licences would end up in the most productive use. Ofcom (and all other regulators around the world) failed to implement clear property rights and remove all the effective impediments to trading. They then compensated by focusing on auctions to try to get the initial distribution as correct as possible and pricing to provide the economic pressure that trading was failing to deliver. This was not a viable way to deliver a fully functioning spectrum market and instead the result was closer to command & control with additional fees for auctions and pricing.

Annual Licence Fees (ALFs) should have been a transitory tool, used as markets were becoming established and then removed when the Wireless Telegraphy (Mobile Spectrum Trading) Regulations 2011 came into force. Instead, they became a permanent feature, likely inhibiting economic gains.

## 7.6 Overall conclusions

There has been a widespread assumption that the benefits from the economic spectrum efficiency gains from the market approach have outweighed the £27.5 billion cost to the industry from auction fees. Our finding is that the economic spectrum efficiency gains are invisible on the benefits side. On the cost side has to be added spectrum pricing through Annual Licence Fees that should have been abolished in 2011 and the unintended collateral damage done to the quality of the mobile infrastructure.

*We have not found any clear rationale or benefits for running spectrum management on this pseudo-market approach. It was the reason for choosing the book title of "Emperor Ofcom's new clothes". Its spectrum efficiency benefits are invisible. We believe this to be a positive conclusion in allowing the UK to unchain itself from the failed market approach. Why this is important is that we will show in Part 2 that there is a new river to be leapt over to arrive at more pro-investment regulatory approach and leaving one foot on the departing bank is never a good idea.*

In the next part we reveal that making the optimal use of licensed mobile spectrum takes spectrum regulation along the path of maximising the performance of the critical national mobile infrastructure the spectrum is currently being used for. We show it will deliver outcomes better aligned with what the UK needs over the coming even more challenging 20 years – and this may be of wider international interest, as several other countries are likely to be in the same place. Whilst the focus in Part 2 is on licensed mobile spectrum for public infrastructure, we also embrace lightly licensed and unlicensed applications that compete and complement licensed mobile spectrum use at the edges, including mobile satellites.

# Part 2

# A better future beckons

# 8 The case for the alternative to the market-based approach for licensed mobile spectrum

## 8.1 The prime purpose of a mobile infrastructure will be better served by improving its essential quality of coverage

When mobile networks began, they were a speculative commercial venture addressing a minority customer need. They then turned into a service for a mass consumer market. Today they have become indispensable to the lives of consumers, citizens, commerce, and Society. Reliable connectivity is now crucial as is resilience and security. This has been recognised by the UK Government who classify mobile networks as part of the Critical National Infrastructure[18].

But the essential quality of coverage from the UK's national mobile infrastructure is in a poor state, a legacy in part, down to the market approach to spectrum policy. This has been partly obscured by the Government, Ofcom and industry defining mobile coverage just in terms of "basic connectivity". What is required today is a consistent essential quality of coverage across the entire country. By "Essential Quality of Coverage" we mean that there are not only basic mobile connections available but also sufficient data capacity to support all concurrent active users and their applications, ensuring each user experience is seamless and uninterrupted. Implicit in this is meeting rising expectation for a "guaranteed" connectivity rather than the "best endeavour" found today over many parts of the country.

---

[18] See, for example, the Government's Wireless 2030 publication which states "Mobile networks have become critical national infrastructure because of the vital public service applications they underpin." at https://www.gov.uk/government/publications/wireless-2030/wireless-2030.

We note that how this essential quality of coverage is defined and measured will be critical, and that in the past lax measures have resulted in published coverage maps not being reflected in the reality of consumer experience. Ofcom, as an independent body, needs to be given the responsibility for defining more effective measures and reporting on them. Crowd-sourced measurements could make up much of the verification since these are directly representative of the user experience and supplemented with other measurements in places.

*Conclusion: The way mobile coverage is defined needs to change from "coverage" of just basic connectivity to the "essential quality of coverage". Such enhanced quality of coverage will require fresh investment to deliver at scale.*

## 8.2    *What a better national mobile infrastructure should look like.*

The early 5G visionaries led the media to believe that the laws of economics, and even the laws of physics, could be suspended. It gave rise to the myth that Gb/s data connectivity could be available everywhere. The encounter with reality exposed two broad directions of travel for the future of mobile and that choice of directions remain valid for the coming 6G era:

1.  *Ever higher data speeds* - The path followed over the past 40 years is every new generation of mobile technology delivering a big leap in peak user data speeds. This inevitably leads to a shrinkage of mobile coverage where the higher speeds are available. The next big leap in user data speeds takes it into the Gb/s ranges. It involves the densification of small cells. The investment required to expand such coverage across very wide areas becomes huge. Therefore, *the cumulative coverage* for a Gb/s goal is unlikely to ever exceed a few percent of the UK landmass.

2.  *Extending the essential quality of coverage universally* - The opposite direction of travel is to go for extending the essential quality of coverage universally ie the minimum that could eventually be delivered to every corner of the UK. The same laws of physics apply. This time a guaranteed minimum data speed can only realistically be in single or low double-digit numbers. We have taken a figure of a guaranteed 10

Mb/s as a placeholder. This allows streaming video at high quality and is a rate where Internet browsing, and other applications are generally limited by factors other than the mobile network. Even that rate may be an economic stretch too far, even over a 20-year time horizon, and studies will be needed before any goal may be set by the Government.

There are, of course, a range of intermediate coverage goals a government could set. For example, raising the essential quality of coverage along every road (right down to minor roads) and every rail line in the country. This may be a sensible milestone on the way to an essential quality of coverage eventually being universal.

*Conclusion: If the country must choose between these two very different directions of travel for the future evolution of mobile access networks, a minimum of 10Mbits/s available universally would deliver the most overall benefit. We present the case for this in the next section.*

## 8.3 The case for extending the essential quality of coverage universally

Infrastructure planning has long lead times, and it is seldom possible to find "evidence" of demand for something that does not yet exist. Instead, there is reliance on economic studies. While there are many publications[19] that note how important mobile communications are to quality of life and productivity we have found a few that aim to quantify this into a cost-benefit for the nation:

- A report by Analysys Masons[20] for DSIT found £8.5bn additional value added for rural industries alone.

---

[19] For example, see the UK Government publication https://www.gov.uk/government/publications/benefits-of-rural-mobile-coverage/benefits-of-rural-mobile-coverage and Ofcom publication https://www.ofcom.org.uk/__data/assets/pdf_file/0017/120455/advice-government-improving-mobile-coverage.pdf

[20] https://assets.publishing.service.gov.uk/government/uploads/system/uploads/attachment_data/file/1147979/realising_the_benefits_of_5G.pdf See Fig 8.4

- A report commissioned by Vodafone[21] found £65bn productivity improvements in the rural economy from better mobile networks.
- A recent 2023 study for mobile deployment in Scotland[22] concluded that investment in rural mobile coverage can be readily justified in terms of the benefits delivered.

However, all such forward-looking economic studies must make assumptions of what is plausible and then seek to dimension them. Dimensioning productivity gains are notoriously difficult for many parts of the economy. Thus, the strength of the productivity case may be better judged by going straight to the assumptions and the plausibility of whether the gains will come about.

### 8.3.1 Quality of mobile coverage driving national productivity gains

Below we give five examples where we believe a higher universal essential quality of coverage would deliver higher national productivity:

- In highly competitive national and international markets "time to market" is crucial. And crucial to that is getting the right information quickly to decision makers and those decisions communicated quickly down the line to those who will action them. Mobile connectivity plays a role in this for distributed staff, where many may be working from home, visiting customers/suppliers or on the move. Ensuring a guaranteed essential quality of coverage everywhere will lead to the time equivalent of a substantial accumulated productivity gain across the economy.
- This becomes even more fruitful with the expected rapid diffusion of AI into business processes intended to optimise business performance in real time.
- Hybrid working is becoming embedded. Often staff are no longer in the same building at the same time. Home working, offering flexible hours,

---

[21] https://news.virginmediao2.co.uk/wp-content/uploads/2023/07/VMO2-Great-Rural-Revival-Report.pdf

[22] https://www.farrpoint.com/uploads/store/mediaupload/1062/file/FarrPoint_rural_comm unity_study_2023.pdf

is good for those tasks only requiring a solo effort but there is an inevitable productivity loss when a team effort is involved. A guaranteed minimum data speed access supporting video-based team meetings contributes to retrieving some of that productivity loss.

- The UK has a huge number of SME's and sole entrepreneurs. The smaller the enterprise the more personal productivity gates economic output. An always connected smartphone (from a guaranteed universal data speed) will directly enhance that personal productivity.

- Our analysis of the driverless car revolution (we explore in the next section) would mean tens of millions of productive hours can be captured though a guaranteed essential quality of coverage along all roads where this is authorised.

*Conclusion: The two that stand out as particularly compelling are the small company/sole trader productivity gains (where a mass of anecdotal evidence exists going all the way back to the high uptake of early mobile phones by plumbers, carpenters, and electricians etc) and, into the future, with productivity gains that will be there to be captured from the driverless car revolution.*

The latter has had least attention, and we believe is most likely to catch out infrastructure planners. For this reason, we examine the impact of autonomous vehicles in more depth in the next section.

## 8.3.2 Autonomous cars, productivity gains and a surge in mobile data demand

Cars are becoming increasingly autonomous. Many cars now being sold can maintain their position in a lane and keep a safe distance from the car in front. Some can change lanes on motorways and similar. At the extreme, there are fully autonomous "robo-taxis" in some US cities now entering commercial operation.

We do not under-estimate the difficulties of implementing autonomous cars and certainly do not expect fully autonomous vehicles, with no need whatsoever for a driver, to be in widespread use in the UK, or other developed countries, in the next decade or two.

However, the evidence is coming together that by around 2035 a large fraction of cars, perhaps the majority, could be self-driving outside of urban areas on designated roads:

- Legislation to allow it already exists in other countries and in the UK is imminent.
- Similarly, suitable highways where it is permitted have started to be designated.
- The technology already exists in cars like Tesla and others, so the installed base of enabled cars is starting to build up.
- As the higher safety record for autonomous driving becomes clearer, insurance premiums are likely to be lower for those that utilise it.

What is timely for the Government, Ofcom and the MNOs is to look well ahead at the implications for data capacity demand on mobile networks covering the likely designated routes. These could ultimately reach 30,000 km of roads or perhaps more. Many of those routes traverse large areas of countryside currently not generating high levels of data traffic. So it would be prudent to anticipate now what impact driverless cars are likely to have on future mobile network capacity needs.

Many have suggested that autonomous cars will require high-speed wireless connectivity to function, or that they will be uploading vast amounts of data daily. This seems to us unlikely in terms of being able to function – an autonomous car will clearly need to work well even without connectivity and hence cannot rely on it. And autonomous cars have functioned so far without needing vast data uploads so it is unclear why they would be needed in future. That said cars that have an accurate internal map of the current road circumstances, traffic levels and emerging incidents can much more quickly route away from trouble or congestion.

Critically, however, it is not just the cars needing data connectivity, drivers inside them, liberated from the need to drive their cars, will do what many passengers do – use their phones, laptops, or screens in the car, for work and entertainment. The car would be a good place to watch video which is one of the most bandwidth-intensive applications. Essentially, what is today occasional hands-free telephone calls could become a connection to the broadband Internet doing things the drivers might have been doing over the broadband Internet at home or at the office.

Data volumes in many of the mobile cells currently having light traffic loading could change dramatically – even by as much as an order of magnitude. We see this as near certain. Whilst 2035 seems a long way away, significantly bolstering the data capacity along the eventual 30,000 km of highways may take a great deal longer. The productivity gains and economic value in providing this capacity suggest planning for it now could be just in time.

Of course, autonomous cars could develop further to be able to drive in urban areas. Manufacturers might send or receive much more data from the vehicle to assist its operation. Hence, we believe that our expectations here are a lower bound on the loading that will appear on the mobile networks.

### 8.3.3   Societal Gains

The societal value of better universal essential quality of coverage is widely understood, including in the areas of health and personal security. What is yet to unfold is the role of mobile connectivity in dealing with the various national threats such as extreme weather events from climate change, pandemics, impending power outages and terrorist activities. Mobile cell broadcasts of local and national warnings are in still in their infancy.

These life-threatening events can occur in remote locations that are not an economic priority, even for basic mobile connectivity. One of the national policy dilemmas has always been the appropriate level of insurance for low probability events with high destructive capacity. What now needs to be factored in is the likelihood that these extreme events occur with higher frequency anywhere.

*Conclusion: Whilst the needs are clear from all the above illustrative examples, the critical question therefore becomes how a limited investment pot can be stretched to embrace all these needs across the greatest extent of the country.*

## 8.4   The new economic role for mobile spectrum regulation

All the UK's utilities infrastructures, which now includes mobile broadband networks, have been suffering from under-investments over recent years. The problem of our time is how to catch up when economic conditions are now far more challenging. In the particular case for upgrading the quality of universal mobile coverage the issues are:

- The MNO's investment capacity is already at full stretch and "the market" is unlikely to roll out capacity relief much beyond 30% of the UK.
- The very high level of the national debt severely constrains any taxpayer subsidies in the foreseeable future to make up for this market failure.

Public and regulatory policies towards a regulated utility always play a critical role in what the private sector finds viable to invest in.

*We know a new infrastructure quality led approach to licensed mobile spectrum policy can change the economics of delivering the essential quality of coverage at scale. The question is whether it can be transformational. We are confident it can be.*

In the next section we describe the new approach and later in Chapter 9 we show, through illustrative examples, that it has the potential to be transformational.

## 8.5   Defining a new infrastructure quality driven approach to licensed mobile spectrum policy

### 8.5.1   Principles of a new infrastructure quality driven approach to licensed mobile spectrum regulation

The gains to the country could be substantial from a new revolution in licensed mobile spectrum policy designed around the following five principles:

- Redefining the optimal use of the spectrum for the country as seeking *"the best infrastructure outcome"* meeting the needs of consumers, citizens, society, and the economy *"for the spectrum being used"*. This means, in practice, that mobile spectrum regulation can no longer be *financially extractive*. There can be spectrum auctions and annual licence fees, but optimal use of the spectrum means paying what is due through extending the essential quality of coverage.

- Aligning Ofcom's exercise of its licensed mobile spectrum powers with the Government's long-term wireless infrastructure goals.
- The Government, Ofcom, and the MNOs arriving at a new consensus on the boundaries between network competition, regulation, and cooperation.
- What network competition fails to deliver must be delivered through new "cooperation dynamics". In this, profitable MNOs are a national asset.
- Having mobile policy/regulations tailored to the prevailing economic/ demographic circumstances in various zones of the country (we believe that there are three distinctive zones).

We have set out the case for the first of these principles in previous sections. We now discuss in more detail the other four.

### 8.5.2 Aligning Government infrastructure goals with Ofcom's exercise of licensed mobile spectrum policy

Crucial to the delivery of this next revolution is redefining the policy power relationship between the Government and Ofcom for mobile spectrum. Currently, one of the reasons the UK's mobile regulatory framework is falling short in advancing the nation's infrastructure objectives is due to the nature of the formal separation between the Government and Ofcom for spectrum policy.

Figure 7 illustrates what needs to change. Achieving the right policy power balance between the Government and Ofcom could be as simple as legislating to add a new principal duty on Ofcom to deliver the Government's long-term infrastructure goals.

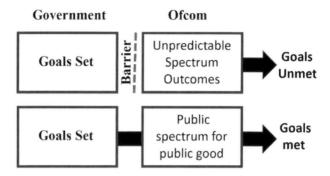

Figure 7– Redefining the policy power relationship that aligns Ofcom's mobile spectrum policy with the Government's infrastructure goals.

This simple legislative spectrum policy power rebalancing would incur the least disruptive institutional change whilst best ensuring the UK has a national wireless infrastructure delivering the essential quality of coverage needed across the UK to increase productivity and social wellbeing.

The assumption was made in 2003 that the "stability" needed for the industry to invest required a structure that would tend to resist change. But in the very rapidly changing world, described in Chapter 6, it has had the effect of not keeping up with changes fast enough. It has left our MNOs with a weak capacity to invest. It is almost guaranteed the next 20 years will bring even more far-reaching global changes that the UK cannot insulate itself from. The confidence to invest will be far more assured by a better-balanced regulatory framework in which the regulator seeks optimal outcomes that can deliver the Government's national infrastructure goals, sustain profitable MNOs, and ensure affordable prices for consumers.

The role of the government in setting long-term goals for our national infrastructure can, of itself, be very powerful in aligning the energies within the various contributing private and public entities behind the shared goals.

### 8.5.3    A new consensus

A new consensus is needed on the optimal boundaries between competition, regulation, and cooperation.

- Governments must look beyond the next General Election in setting the UK's mobile infrastructure goals.
- Ofcom need to extend their passion for looking after the consumer's interests to looking after the nation's interest in a better universal mobile quality of coverage. Whilst "technology neutrality" was central to "the market approach", that has now to be redefined where specific new standardised technologies can deliver superior spectrum, energy, and coverage efficiencies. The national benefits will be delivered much faster with a favourable regulatory tail wind behind them.
- Finally, MNOs have been comfortable for decades in cooperating with each other over research and technical standards without endangering effective competition. Cooperation over spectrum usage (not for its own sake but where there is mutual benefit) needs to be brought into that comfort zone.

That is easier said than done. But it can be done.

### 8.5.4 What competition fails to deliver must be delivered through cooperation dynamics

Mobile retail competition has remained intense. It has delivered very low consumer prices, even to an extent of limiting investment. The situation has been quite different for mobile infrastructure competition intensity. Partly because of the intensity of retail competition, infrastructure competition intensity has been on a declining curve from 3G to 5G. Allowing infrastructure sharing over a decade ago began the slide. Network-based competition now influences investment only to the extent that an MNO feels pressure not to be too far behind (comparative competition).

This entanglement of retail and network competition has been a headache for competition regulators. MNO consolidation will help reduce the retail competitive intensity, improve MNOs' finances, and hence stop the further slide in their capacity to invest that has characterised the past ten years. But the willingness to invest in what has become a utility business is another matter.

Therefore, a fundamental question for policy makers is how innovation and more investment, from what have become utilities, are going to be galvanised in a market of long-term declining intensity of infrastructure competition between the MNOs?

We do not agree with those who argue that an infrastructure monopoly is the right answer. There is a benefit to be had from comparative competition. Instead, we propose the shortfall left by weakening network competition should be filled with "cooperative dynamics" which delivers a mutual benefit and contributes to the shared infrastructure goals. That has already happened with the shared rural network, where all four MNOs work together to build a single network that they share and there are a myriad of lower cost and more flexible cooperation opportunities. "Cooperation" has been in the DNA of the telecommunications industry since its inception.

However, fostering cooperative dynamics will be new for a regulator that has grown up to rely entirely on competition. Just as in the early 80's policy makers had to learn how to introduce competition into what hitherto was regarded as a natural monopoly, so today's generation of policy makers will have to learn the art of "cooperative dynamics" with the tools at their disposal, including the respect within which the industry holds the regulator and government. Opportunities to do that in mobile spectrum policy are substantial. We provide some illustrative examples later in section 9.3.

The optimum regulatory framework will be the one that gets the best mix possible of competition and cooperation.

### 8.5.5 High performing regulation can only be achieved when regulation is tailored to the prevailing economic circumstances

A high performing regulatory framework can only be achieved by optimising the regulatory policy to the economic circumstances prevailing in various parts of the country. If, across the country, there are three distinct economic/demographic circumstances, there needs to be three tailored regulatory frameworks.

Section 9.1 identifies the three distinct prevailing economic conditions and looks at the policies needed for each:

1. Areas where the competitive market can deliver continuously improving quality of mobile coverage.
2. Areas where regulatory assistance is required to create the conditions to make investing viable. We provide a rich set of examples that demonstrate how spectrum policy can achieve this.
3. Areas where there is no economic case for investing. These areas are where a case for a public subsidy on societal grounds rests with the Government. Today public finances are at full stretch so it may not be possible to immediately invest. Deferring action may be beneficial in allowing time for more cost-efficient coverage technologies to mature such as high-altitude platforms.

*Conclusion:    We have set out the next revolution in licensed mobile spectrum policy that we believe is the only one that can, at the same time: improve economic spectrum efficiency; better align Government infrastructure ambitions and Ofcom spectrum policy; solve the problem of declining network competition intensity; secure a new more productive boundary between network competition, regulation, and cooperation; and better map regulatory policies to demographic/economic circumstances. This can all be accomplished with the least institutional and industrial disruption.*

# 9 The next revolution in the management of licensed mobile spectrum

In this chapter we get into more detail and provide a rich list of illustrative examples to show the potential of spectrum policy for driving transformative economic change. We have added a few examples falling outside of mobile spectrum policy where we believe these to be important and part of the role of the Government or regulator.

We then turn our attention to lightly licensed spectrum (including satellites) and unlicensed spectrum. We have embraced these in the in the scope of the book because their uses compete and complement licensed mobile spectrum use. These two topics are covered in Chapters 10 and 11.

We see this new revolutionary approach as meeting the national needs over the next 20 years. However, in Chapter 12 we probe what may lay beyond 20 years for mobile spectrum policy. This long view provides confidence that the new direction of travel is aligned with plausible possibilities we can already discern at that distance.

## 9.1 In the new revolution "three sizes fit all"

Part 1 has shown the market approach to spectrum has failed to enable repurposing of spectrum from other uses to mobile. Its effect today can, at best, only shuffle spectrum between competitors in the same use. Competition policy has blocked all but the most minor shuffling. On the other hand, it can have a haphazard impact on the performance of a vital national infrastructure due to the unpredictable outcomes of any market approach. Its financially extractive nature has been applied to an industry already stressed through other factors and can only have been unhelpful.

This leads to a conclusion that there is now only one approach to mobile spectrum regulation that can drive more optimal use of the spectrum that is now inextricably tied to a critical national infrastructure. That is for spectrum policy to be directed at enhancing the performance of that infrastructure. We term this new regulatory approach *"infrastructure quality driven"* mobile spectrum regulation.

At the outset the mobile regulator treated the UK as one entity and had one national regulatory set of rules applying everywhere. It was "one size fits all". But it didn't. There were parts of the country where infrastructure competition was working well and other parts where the demographics just did not allow it to function. Rural Britain was largely left with no mobile coverage.

This led to a more efficient two regulatory model approach. In rural Britain the new approach allowed network sharing between all competing MNOs with a 50% Government subsidy. The Shared Rural Network emerged. But its extent and quality reflected the unwillingness of both the MNOs and the Government at the time to invest at scale. It signalled the limitations of this shared taxpayer-MNO funding approach to adequately redress even the current basic mobile connectivity failings.

Since then, a second market failure has surfaced in the supply of sufficient quality of coverage ie the wide diffusion of sufficient data capacity across the country. This is what 5G enhance mobile broadband was supposed to deliver. But MNOs have struggled to roll out 5G technology in wide bandwidth at sufficient scale to provide enough capacity where there is already basic coverage.

A White Paper from the University of Surrey 5G/6GIC on mobile regulation[23] identified one of the reasons. There was no longer an alignment between the coverage that was commercially viable for the MNOs financed from their access fee revenues alone and the coverage that was economically optimal for the country, considering the values from the mobile network's externalities (productivity gains and over the top services). It has also not been a government priority for an injection of taxpayer subsidy to redress this new market failure.

---

[23] University of Surrey White Paper on mobile regulation in process of publication. https://www.surrey.ac.uk/institute-communication-systems/5g-6g-innovation-centre/white-papers

The University of Surrey went on to conclude that there were now three very distinct demographic economic zones, and a high performing mobile regulation framework was now only possible if there were three regulatory frameworks each optimised to the economic conditions in each of the zones. Figure 8 illustrates these three distinctive essential quality coverage economic zones.

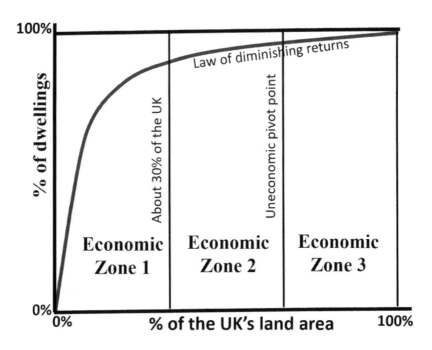

Figure 8 – The UK broken into three zones with very different cost of coverage conditions and thus different investment incentives

The steep part of the curve represents the easy areas to cover. One tall tower on a high spot in London will quickly be heavily loaded with traffic. At the other end of the curve labelled "the law of diminishing returns" is where ever larger numbers of towers are picking up ever less traffic. Towers in the most remote areas may only get traffic from occasional ramblers. Such towers will generate no additional revenue for the MNOs, but the MNOs will incur additional costs in providing the service.

Thus a "universal coverage" ambition must be sub-divided into three distinctive economic or societal zones:

- Zone 1 reflects "the MNO business investment case" that rests on access fees alone. The roll out of wide bandwidth services by the MNOs is only likely to reach the bend in the curve. The extra cost of coverage much beyond the bend will never be recovered by extra access fees.

- Zone 2 we term "The national economic investment case." If the economic value to the country of all the "over the top" services and productivity gains were to be added into the business case, it would very likely justify significantly more geographic coverage[24]. But none of these externalities can be monetised by the MNOs and captured in the MNO business case. We have a significant area of the country (laying between dense urban and rural and criss-crossed with many road and rail links) with a broadband network needing more capacity but where neither MNOs nor Government currently see as their role to invest in upgrading the capacity and Ofcom do not see it as their duty to use their policy levers to make it happen; although they do accept that better coverage is needed[25]. This is the zone where the economics could be transformed by a pro-investment spectrum policy approach.

- Zone 3 "The societal value case." A point will be reached where no further coverage can be justified purely on economic grounds. But there may be political reasons to complete the universal essential quality of coverage, such as digital inclusion, that warrants a public subsidy. While that subsidy currently looks unaffordable, better times may well be ahead. On the horizon are direct satellite to smartphones and high-altitude platforms as discussed later in this chapter. These could dramatically reduce the cost of upgrading deeply rural coverage.

The shape of the curve is believed to be representative, but the numbers are illustrative. The numbers on the curve in Figure 8 may appear significantly

---

[24] As discussed in Chapter 8, further study is needed here, but reports such as https://www.farrpoint.com/uploads/store/mediaupload/1062/file/FarrPoint_rural_comm unity_study_2023.pdf would strongly suggest this is the case.

[25] https://www.ofcom.org.uk/__data/assets/pdf_file/0017/120455/advice-government-improving-mobile-coverage.pdf

different from historic and current reported coverage numbers - for example Ofcom suggest that there is coverage of around 99% of the population and 90% of the landmass. However, as mentioned previously, they are related only to the most basic connectivity.

*Conclusion: The future requires a very different criteria for coverage – one where there is sufficient capacity and signal quality to guarantee a government specified essential minimum data rate (eg 10Mbits/s) to all those in the cell that want it. Thus, the new focus is on "essential quality of coverage". We show in the next section that the competitive market is likely to deliver an essential quality of coverage only up to around 30% of the UK landmass. This exposes the need to break the UK up into three economic/demographic zones each with its own distinctive regulatory policy approach.*

We will now look in more detail into each of these three zones:

## 9.2 Economic Zone 1 - The geographic area where mobile competition will deliver ever improving essential quality of mobile coverage.

### 9.2.1 What the competitive market is likely to deliver

The evidence over the past 20 years points to a coverage of around a third of the country (or where 90% of the population live) where the competitive mobile market is likely to deliver the essential quality of coverage. This would take it to just beyond the bend in the curve in Figure **8** and hence, beyond this, the business case for investment becoming ever weaker.

There may be a spread of outcomes between different MNOs (with geographic variations), but competition can be relied upon to eventually lead to broadly comparable outcomes in the use of spectrum able to accommodate wide bandwidths and cell splitting when spectrum capacity is at its local limits.

Zone 1 is the easiest to also deliver data rates far more than 10 Mb/s and that is the case today. Some envisage Gb/s rates in a future 6G era. It is worth a quick digression as there are some comparable regulatory issues worth noting in passing.

Having some significant commercial islands of such exceptional data speeds and capacity could be useful in promoting innovations and finding out if there is a demand for local Gbits/s connectivity. If, from this, there is then the Government may need to step in to improve the economics of urban dense small cell clusters. What might this involve?

An obvious place to attach small cell antenna is on streetlight structures. They are in the right place, have the right height, power is on hand and fibre optical cables are likely to be running alongside. But the ownership of the lamp posts and fibre, and the prices they charge the MNOs for small cell use will determine whether the business case works. If it does not, there is a case for Government intervention. Not to do so will be a barrier to meeting capacity demands. Also, the MNOs erecting their own structures in quantity will "industrialise" the leafy suburban street views with clutters of lamp post sized masts. Such an environmental impact can be avoided if existing structures, like streetlights, are required to be used.

### 9.2.2   What of the future of the MNOs

As Zone 1 is being defined as where the competitive market is most likely to function in raising the essential quality of coverage, a question arises - what of the future of the MNOs and what future do they see for themselves? The MNOs' journey has been in two halves. The first two decades has been a growth story, with strong interest in entering the network market and ready access to capital. The second two decades have seen their business models come under ever greater stress, with MNOs wanting to leave the market and it is now very tough to attract capital to fund new technology investment cycles. But the tide in their fortunes may be turning again. The Government is recognising a common thread across all of the UK utilities, that their regulatory frameworks have turned out not to be sufficiently pro-investment, adversely affecting economic growth. Our new revolution in licensed mobile spectrum policy aligns with this new thinking. The country needs MNOs to become a success story in the pivotal role they will continue to play over the next twenty years.

*Conclusion: The competitive market is likely to deliver the essential quality of coverage over about a third of the country. For this to happen, the country needs profitable MNOs. They are also a national asset with much more to contribute to areas like skills training, research and potentially helpful to a national industrial policy, such as using their purchasing power to pull through innovative technology start-ups.*

## 9.3 Economic Zone 2 - Where spectrum policy intervention is required to make essential quality of coverage improvements economically viable

Left to the status quo, there is likely to be little upgrading in the essential quality of coverage in this zone. The broad aim for a new approach is for Ofcom to use its spectrum policy powers to transform the economics of a higher quality of coverage. In this way the enhancements in capacity become viable for private sector investments right up to the line shown in Figure 8 as the uneconomic pivot point. There are a lot of economic and technical studies to be done to define where exactly this line occurs. That needs to await the evaluation by a re-focussed Ofcom deciding for itself which tools are appropriate and to what practical limit.

The extra investments may not only come from the MNOs. There may be possibilities to harness the investments of others in a way that the resulting coverage can be integrated seamlessly with MNO coverage. We come to this later. There may be other willing investors to provide coverage at very specific locations in this zone, along the lines envisaged in the 2018 DCMS Future Telecoms Infrastructure Review[26] under the title of "the Market Expansion Model". There is also scope to make more efficient use existing spectrum holdings that can stave off needing new investments in cell splitting. Anything that can cut the cost of providing the essential quality of coverage will allow more such coverage for the same investment.

We set out to show, through a range of examples, how spectrum policy can drive transformational change in the Zone 2 economics of coverage.

---

[26] https://www.gov.uk/government/publications/future-telecoms-infrastructure-review

There are four broad ways of achieving this:

1. Find new revenue streams.
2. Exchange of new spectrum for new commitments.
3. Secure efficiency gains.
4. Cut costs.

These are covered in the next four sections.

The intention is not to hold up any example as a game changer. Nor do we claim novelty – some of these ideas have been suggested many years ago but not implemented. It is also far from an exhaustive list. What these examples are intended to show is that, taken together with other ideas Ofcom themselves and others will no doubt come up with, the new approach is both credible and potentially transformational.

## 9.3.1 New revenue streams

In this section we set out the following non-exclusive approaches to delivering additional revenue:

- Repurposing annual licence fees.
- National roaming as a premium service.
- Charging large content providers a carriage fee.
- Harnessing a public procurement contribution

### 9.3.1.1 Repurposing the Annual Licence Fees

The Government (DSIT) in their thoughtful March 2023 Spectrum Statement[27] asked Ofcom to investigate more pro-investment alternatives to their spectrum pricing status quo. The industry has been active through the Spectrum Policy Forum in seeking a more enlightened approach. There were differing views among the MNOs. The optimists wanted to see annual fees abolished and keep the money. The realists did not believe the Treasury would accept this and a more credible "ask" was for the money to be repurposed to invest in gaps in coverage along road and rail links. An alternative idea was to fund improving

---

[27] https://www.gov.uk/government/publications/spectrum-statement/spectrum-statement

battery back-up at base stations to make networks more resilient. Both deliver improvements in economic spectrum efficiency and therefore can be linked directly to Ofcom's powers to make optimal use of the spectrum.

There are several ways this could be done. One, just for illustrative purposes, is for Ofcom to be the repository of data of all the networks' coverage and capacity weak spots. It is not difficult to cost out the solution for each. Then they are put in order of cost benefit and MNOs can select which they will commit to such that the combined cost totals to the Annual Licence Fee due.

Applying the current annual licence fee levels (around £300m in 2022) to infrastructure improvements over the next 20 years would total a £6 billion investment. That would be the equivalent of adding six new Shared Rural Networks. It also aligns with Ofcom estimates[28] of the cost of delivering 100% basic UK coverage.

9.3.1.2    National Roaming as a new premium service

The one thing that has unified all MNOs since 1985 is their strong opposition to national roaming. A national roaming condition was in the very first cellular mobile licences to retrieve an estimated 18% spectrum efficiency loss through partitioning the spectrum between two competing MNOs. One of the few things that Cellnet and Vodafone agreed upon was to lobby the new regulator, Oftel, to have it taken out. They argued it would stifle competition to extend mobile coverage. The regulator agreed. The most recent argument with the Government over national roaming showed opposition to a national roaming obligation remains very strong.

Our research showed three principal reasons for this more recent opposition to a measure that would have offset the weakness of coverage competition to fill coverage not spots.

1.   EE felt that this would remove one of their main competitive advantages of better national coverage. But surprisingly their

---

[28] https://www.ofcom.org.uk/__data/assets/pdf_file/0017/120455/advice-government-improving-mobile-coverage.pdf

competitors were not so keen to see EE losing this advantage as to want to embrace national roaming.

2. MNOs were worried about losing control of their costs. As their customers wandered onto EE's network, they would have to pay roaming charges and their operating costs would go up. The concern was a loss of control of their cost base.

3. The third reason was the consequences if one of the networks were to have a catastrophic failure. The sudden roaming of 10 million consumers onto the other surviving networks could saturate them to the point of nobody having any service anywhere[29]. It would not be unlike a denial-of-service attack that happens on the Internet but in this case accidentally.

Here we suggest a possible new approach to national roaming that might overcome these issues. Previously, everyone has assumed that national roaming must be a free entitlement for everyone. The benefits to consumers would be the gift equivalent to a free subscription to all the other networks. To most of the MNOs it was yet another regulatory raid on their profitability.

Instead, we propose national roaming would become a premium subscription service aimed at those who valued better coverage and reliability the most. Then it becomes almost "free money" for MNOs to distribute between profit and investment. A subscription service removes the loss of control of costs from a usage-based model. The service can have its own range of data caps to ensure demand on the networks was fair.

The offer has potential to succeed as a premium subscription service for those depending upon good mobile connectivity. The benefits would be significant as it fills in all those areas where not all MNOs are present at a stroke and the user's home network is backed up by the other networks in the event of failure. The cost falls only on those able to afford it. This may limit the level of take up to a small minority. But that is also a benefit in the event of a catastrophic failure of one of the networks. The other networks are better able to handle the sudden increase in traffic.

---

[29] We note that approaches could be used to control loading such as throttling users and temporarily changing some network parameters.

As it makes money it should not need coercive powers. It is an example of where "orchestration" and a nod from the competition regulator might be all that is needed.

### 9.3.1.3    Charging the giant application providers a carriage fee

This is a hugely polarising issue. It would be a distraction from the purpose of this book to come down on one side or the other. But it is a debate that is likely to run and run, so we set down our views of the pros and cons.

The arguments for the MNOs charging a carriage fee are:

- It would mean that those generating large content currently would face incentives to minimise their data flows over bandwidth limited networks or financially contribute to lifting the limits.
- There are a relatively small number of large content providers who originate perhaps 50% of all mobile traffic making it feasible.
- There could be an industrial policy advantage were UK public service broadcasters to be exempt from the charge.

The arguments against the MNOs charging a carriage fee are:

- Some of the giant application providers have huge market power and would not hesitate to play off one MNO against another. So there is doubt if it can be made to stick.
- An outcome could emerge where not only the MNOs did not secure any meaningful revenue but some of the most popular content was withheld by the powerful tech companies.
- If it were to be allowed, Ofcom may have to set the price, so the MNOs were not played off against each another. Ofcom would then find themselves between the MNOs on one side and the big tech companies and consumer groups on the other. In that fight the revenue potential to the MNOs that emerges may be relatively small.

The balance of probabilities is that it is the least likely of the potential new revenue sources to materialise in the foreseeable future.

### 9.3.1.4    Harnessing a public procurement contribution

This possibility may appear to be going "off-piste" from the use of licensed spectrum policy. But since the new approach has the Government as a stakeholder in Ofcom's success, an approach to Government to use its public procurement powers to catalyse a new quality of coverage solution is just another tool in the toolbox. For example, providing public mobile coverage inside of public buildings using an advanced technology solution could be kick-started through the Government seeking competitive bids from MNOs, where one of the qualifying criteria might be the MNOs commitment to do the same in some large commercial complexes. Beyond the Government, as purchasers of essential quality of coverage are local authorities and health authorities,

### 9.3.2    Exchange of new spectrum for new commitments

New spectrum use in profitable areas can be made to subsidise its use in unprofitable areas. That is essentially what a successful coverage obligation does. Part One showed the limited success of coverage obligations where their effect was weakened because of the priority being given to the market approach to spectrum auction design. On the other hand, "Cashless" spectrum auctions would deliver a far more effective outcome. In these, bidders bid the infrastructure improvement they are prepared to contract for in exchange for the spectrum. It is a variant of coverage obligations but drawing far more investment in infrastructure improvements and can be much better targeted than a blanket coverage obligation. The economic efficiency gain is real as opposed to the invisible gain from the market approach.

As noted earlier, historically it has proven hard to measure and enforce such promises or obligations. We believe that new tools such as crowd-sourced measurements can accurately measure whether commitments are being made, and stage payments and similar used such that the MNOs only receive payment (or credits or similar) after the coverage has been provided and measurements show it is at the required levels.

This possibility needs new spectrum. So where is it to come from and how likely is it for Ofcom to be able to find it?

One of the lessons well learnt by the 5G spectrum community was the economic difference between "coverage" spectrum band and "capacity" spectrum bands. This gave rise to Europe agreeing to three 5G pioneer bands, one offering great capacity but poor coverage, one great coverage and poor capacity and the mid band (3.4-3.8 GHz) providing a mix of both. Figure 9 below illustrates the vast difference between what is in prospect for new "coverage" spectrum versus new "capacity" spectrum.

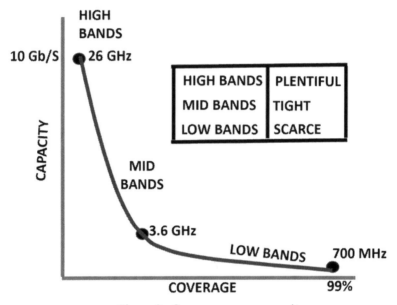

Figure 9– Coverage versus capacity

There is little limit to accessing ever-higher frequencies far above 3.5GHz and heading into THz. Those bands are very good for enhancing capacity but are of very little value in enhancing coverage. Even the value of "capacity" bands will diminish the higher their frequency. This makes mid-band the fertile area to be looking.

It is new lower frequencies that are most valuable for enhancing universal coverage even with limited capacity. Cellular now has spectrum down to 700MHz. Spectrum down to around 500-600MHz would be useful, but below these frequencies, handset antennas become too large, and signals can propagate too far for the spectrum to be useful for cellular by limiting reuse.

The spectrum from around 500-700MHz is used by digital terrestrial television (DTT). This has been a UK success story. Freeview was a great consumer proposition attracting audience sizes that compared very favourably with cable and satellite. But over the last 20 years on-demand streaming services over the fixed and mobile broadband Internet have been consistently growing. A consensus has emerged that linear TV viewing is in long term decline. This has set an expectation among MNOs that eventually all the DTT's 600 MHz spectrum could be made over to them to bolster their limited low band capacity. The Government's present position is that this is a prospect only to be considered after 2034.

Very often things in slow decline can be a long time dying but sometimes they can go into a terminal spiral long before a date officially set. The decline and fall of terrestrial TV channel viewing numbers is likely to be very asymmetrical. As the less-watched channels become uneconomic and cease broadcasting, the costs of the DTT network fall increasingly on the remaining content providers with larger audiences. Eventually they become too great and the network economics collapse resulting in a relatively sudden switch-off. Even before this happens, the steady reduction in channels can lead to the perception that there is nothing worth watching on TV versus the vast choice on-line. This may lead to opportunity for DTT to comprise just the popular TV channels that sustain the value of the DTT proposition and for the earlier transfer of the vacated 600 MHz spectrum to relieve the pressure on mobile low bands.

The tough problem Ofcom has in finding clean mobile spectrum even in the mid band range suggests there may be a need for MNOs to be willing to share spectrum with others. This prospect is expanded upon in the next chapter. Also to be mentioned in passing is sharing between mobile and satellites – a prospect under research study in the 6G network of networks context.

### 9.3.3   Secure efficiency gains

There are many ways that mobile spectrum efficiency could be enhanced including:

- Pooling of spectrum.
- Network re-engineering.
- Network-driven roaming.
- Futuristic spectrum efficient technologies.

9.3.3.1    Spectrum Pooling

There is significant unused MNO spectrum across the UK. The higher the mobile band the more the spectrum is likely to under-used over large areas of the country. But there is even a significant amount of valuable low band spectrum going to waste around remote towers. In semi-urban areas not all MNOs are using their capacity spectrum in the same locations. At those locations there will also be idle spectrum.

MNOs that are present in locations where spectrum is unused are giving their consumers a lower quality of service in busy period than need be the case. They may also have to invest earlier than is needed in cell splitting to generate new capacity. There is a strong self-interest case for MNOs to pool unused spectrum and allow each other to use any spectrum laying nearby unused. It buys the MNO time before having to invest in cell splitting. Consumers get a better quality of service. Nobody is losing anything.

An MNO can always retrieve their unused spectrum by investing to bring it into use. A reasonable period of notice is of mutual interest. That retrieval may occur from time to time but in most cases, particularly in less dense areas of the country, the opportunistic use will be very stable over a very long period, and more so if coupled with the premium national roaming strategy discussed earlier.

In summary, the gain in national economic spectrum efficiency from spectrum pooling could be significant if all the unused spectrum from all the MNOs was to be pooled in an "unused spectrum sharing club" and available to club members to use opportunistically.

If the MNOs were to decide to collectively manage the pooling of unused spectrum in this way, it would be a form of cashless "spectrum trading". In the future this could evolve into an automated approach of dynamics loans and retrievals.

### 9.3.3.2 Reengineering the networks

After 40 years it would be a miracle for everything to have finished in its optimal place:

- The low band spectrum is fragmented, and much efficiency could be gained by de-fragmenting the bands.
- Many towers are coming to the end of their design life. There may be a case to re-locate some of the replacement towers and certainly to add another 10m to their height in sparse locations.
- Some towers would benefit from re-dressing the antenna arrays or changing to more efficient antenna systems. Many are not owned by the MNOs.

The big prize, if a way could be found to do it with minimum disruption to services, would be to sunset the current frequency division technology used across the entire UHF spectrum (600 to 900 MHz) and replace it all with time division technology. This would both remove the many guard bands that are wasted spectrum and allow for the spectrum to be biased towards downlink which sees much more traffic than the uplink. The 600 MHz band could well be the key to this non-disruptive transformation to maintain service during the transitionary process.

Cumulatively there is a huge spectrum efficiency gains there for the taking but it needs investment, and it needs orchestrating. That would be a role for Ofcom in a new infrastructure quality driven licensed mobile spectrum policy.

### 9.3.3.3 Network driven roaming

Where MNOs find themselves on different towers there is a huge efficiency gain in each network being able to hand off a user at their cell edge to a competitor MNO with a much nearer tower. The benefits are symmetrical between MNOs.

A user at the cell edge can consume up to twenty times the capacity needed to support a customer than one that is very close to the tower. Moving users to nearer towers on different networks could collectively increase network capacity many-fold.

This is shown in Figure 10 below where there is a Cell A from one operator and close to the edge of its coverage is a Cell B from another. A user at the very edge of coverage from Cell A only has a relatively limited amount of capacity to access. Whereas if their connection is moved across to Cell B, the user's needs can be served from where the capacity is plentiful.

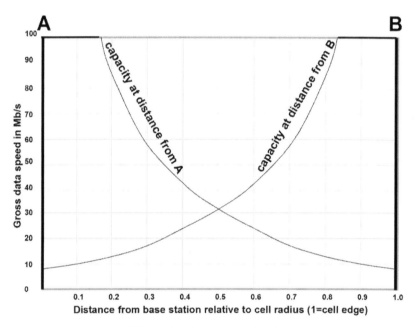

Figure 10 – Gains from network driven roaming

Achieving this would require tight coupling between networks, with shared neighbouring cell lists and the ability to rapidly handoff from one network to another. While technically possible it probably ranks low in likelihood terms in view of the significant cooperation needed to implement it, but the local capacity gains are so substantial as to warrant a mention. In the longer-term research into "cell-less architectures" may achieve even greater benefits from network driven roaming.

### 9.3.3.4 More futuristic techniques

Various technologies being researched include "cell sweeping" which retrieves a lot of lost cell edge capacity, antenna arrays with low side lobes which enhance spectrum sharing and deployment of large intelligent surfaces to reflect signals into coverage holes and saves on the cost of adding active new cells.

There is currently much interest as to whether AI can deliver efficiency gains (and/or cost reductions). AI could analyse individual radio links to see whether there are sets of parameters, for example for the MIMO antennas, which could provide greater capacity, and automatically enhance network operation. It could re-assess optimal levels of interference between any one cell and any other in the network and much more. This remains a research topic and may need to await 6G to be fully realised.

Where more spectrum or coverage efficient technologies emerge, their passage into use might happen faster with a favourably regulatory tail wind.

### 9.3.4 Cutting costs

There are also many ways to cut the cost of improving the essential quality of mobile coverage including:

- Using networks owned by others to expand coverage.
- Using HAPs to deliver lower-cost coverage.
- Having a thin GSM network remain in service.
- Reduce energy costs.
- Reducing base station deployment costs.

A few on this list fall outside of purely mobile spectrum policy and into wider telecoms policy but are included to illustrate that other avenues exist for cutting the cost of high-quality coverage. It also flags where Ofcom might usefully be given new powers.

### 9.3.4.1 The Market Expansion Model

A thoughtful idea to come out of DCMS (now DSIT) to see new investment flows into mobile network infrastructure was their "market expansion model" published in their 2018 Future Telecommunications Infrastructure Review. The proposition was that areas unprofitable to the MNOs would be open to investments from neutral hosts and other enterprises, perhaps with lower overhead business models, to deliver more public mobile coverage and capacity.

The market expansion model has had three problems to solve:

1. Securing more investment in privately provided coverage in public places and public access to private coverage where needed.
2. Securing scale through aggregating privately provided coverage that could be accessible to the public in a managed way.
3. Seamlessly integrating third party provided coverage with MNOs coverage.

a) Securing more investment in privately provided coverage in public places and public access in private coverage where needed

Private entities procuring their own private coverage inside their buildings for their own use already exists at scale with Wi-Fi. There are growing private 5G networks (where control over the interference is seen as critical). The issue is how these private entities might be persuaded to securely open some of their private capacity to the public who are visiting building, especially those with substantial RF screening that blocks signals to and from external MNO networks.

Then there are public spaces without coverage. The hope behind the market expansion model was that private enterprises might step into the market and invest in the provision of mobile coverage (or re-enforcing basic coverage with high-capacity coverage) as a business that has come to be termed "neutral hosts".

There has been some success in a neutral host type approach at locations where crowds congregate, such as sporting venues, where MNOs see coverage as important. A neutral host offer is saving them money by installing one infrastructure and sharing out the cost, as opposed to each MNO implementing their own network.

Self-help groups can sometimes surprise themselves with what can be done in public spirited communities. This may only need a helping hand from Ofcom with advice.

What has not worked is neutral host coverage in areas of less interest to the MNOs. This is because MNOs have been unwilling to pay neutral hosts for that coverage, even at a lower cost than doing it themselves individually. It is a Zone 2 issue.

There may be other routes to better quality of coverage emerging not involving MNOs. Currently the priority of Alt Nets is maximising homes passed. But then attention will turn to persuading more homeowners to connect. They might follow the successful "bundling" model Cable TV companies used. Only this time a low-cost high capacity 5G cell backed onto their fibre would enable them to bundle superior local 5G quality of coverage in with their fibre proposition.

b) Securing scale through aggregating privately provided coverage that could be accessible to the public in a managed way

The best example of a huge opportunity of non-MNO provided mobile coverage available at scale (but currently securely locked away out of reach) is Wi-Fi in our homes and offices. Fifty per cent of UK homes are now passed by full fibre, which implies that a useful cumulative growing percentage of the UK land area is within range of a Wi-Fi signal having 100-500 Mbits/s data capacity behind it. Much of that coverage is indoors but some spills out up to 50m or so around a property and offers the potential of an "inside-out" approach to mobile coverage. It is difficult to put a precise number on it but cumulatively it could add up as much as 5% of the UK land mass depending on the take-up. But it is not accessible. It has been balkanised through encryption security into millions of isolated cells of around 50m radius.

The same potential boost to quality mobile coverage comes from public access to commercial properties. There is 680km$^2$ of commercial floor space across the UK that is likely to be covered by Wi-Fi signals and just emerging are private 5G networks.

Today Wi-Fi in the home and office plays a vital role in lifting a huge quantity of data off wide area mobile networks that simply do not have the bandwidth to take it on. That will continue. But the coverage overspill potential is barely used and visitors to people's homes and third-party commercial premises need a manual exchange of the password to move their use off the wide area mobile networks. Visitors to many commercial buildings, especially those with well screened construction, can find themselves cut off from any mobile connectivity.

All that free Wi-Fi spectrum is not delivering on its full economic spectrum efficiency potential.

Users care about the cost and quality of their mobile services but not about the technology. However, policy makers must be acutely aware of technologies, as the two mainstream technology road maps of cellular and Wi-Fi have very different economics, spectrum cost, industrial eco-systems, regulation, and cooperative dynamics. The big deficit for realising the potential of Wi-Fi to be a part of the universal national coverage asset is the lack of cooperative dynamics.

There have been efforts both here and internationally to form clubs of users willing to grant mutual access to each other's home Wi-Fi routers. But it has never been successfully scaled up into a compelling proposition. There have been good examples on both sides of the Atlantic of cellular mobile operators creating coverage partnerships with commercial building owners. But not yet at scale. This thwarts using Wi-Fi to avoid the large investment in capacity in urban and semi urban areas that the MNOs will otherwise need to make.

What needs to be done technically looks straightforward. The barrier to using Wi-Fi is that most hotspots require manual selection of the router and entry of a password or similar on the first time of use (after that most handsets remember these details and automatically log in). If most Wi-Fi routers were part of a scheme where the same public log-in could be used, then handsets would move onto Wi-Fi whenever they entered almost any building.

This is not a new idea, and there have been many attempts in the past, including the still-existing BT OpenZone arrangement and university EduRoam scheme. They have not gained traction partly because the technology was not there and partly because MNOs had other priorities. Technology has improved, especially with the recent OpenRoaming initiative. A new generation of Wi-Fi routers for home and office with say 20% of their capacity partitioned off as "a neutral host" function could be a game changer. The same for non-industrial private 5G networks.

c) Seamlessly integrating third party provided coverage with MNO provided national coverage

All of the above possibilities have the potential to deliver extensive essential quality of coverage for outgoing traffic. It also provides for incoming over the top calls and message eg via WhatsApp. Missing are incoming conventional mobile calls and SMS text messages that require the cooperation of MNOs to deliver. Ideally, there would be complete integration into the mobile networks so all incoming traffic could be received.

The critical problem to be solved is "the cooperative dynamics" that incentivises comprehensive MNO involvement. They are more likely to engage if it was part of something much bigger in bringing an alignment between the Government's long term infrastructure goals, new duties on Ofcom to incentivise those goals and the MNOs strategies for both surviving as profitable enterprises and delivering the goals.

It would be fair to describe the market expansion model as remaining a great idea, having huge potential but falling into the "all too difficult" category. The benefits are sufficiently as to warrant a bold effort starting with the government setting an over-arching ambition that embraces Wi-Fi and 5G and both outdoors and indoors. Ofcom can then help to get the environment right so that hundreds of individual initiatives can find their own way to slot in their entrepreneurial contributions.

### 9.3.4.2    High Altitude Platforms and satellites

An alternative to the challenges and costs of delivering terrestrial rural networks might be "base stations in the sky".

There are two broad approaches to base stations in the skies – high altitude platforms which fly in the atmosphere and satellites orbiting above the atmosphere. Both are likely to have a role to play.

High altitude platforms (HAPs) represent a broad class of "flying base stations". They could be considered either as very tall telecom towers or very low altitude satellites or somewhere in the middle and some even mobile.

There are many different types of HAPs, broadly:
- Heavier than air:
  - Conventional planes.
  - Unmanned drones, typically fixed wing eg Stratospheric platforms, Aalto Zepher.
- Lighter than air:
  - Tethered balloons eg Softbank Altaeros.
  - Aerostats or dirigibles (balloons that have propulsion), eg Sceye.
  - Free flying balloons, eg Google Loon (discontinued).

HAPs provide a much greater coverage area than conventional cells but smaller than satellites. They tend to have greater capacity than satellites but less than a network of terrestrial cells. Coverage and capacity vary across the different types of HAPs, broadly according to how high they fly, from a few hundred meters for tethered balloons to 20km+ for some drones and aerostats.

As such, their role is in delivering coverage into areas that are too rural for cellular networks but not so deeply rural that there are almost no inhabitants. They could have a role in covering nearly all the UK's rural areas.

The key issue for HAPs is the cost of operation. Maintaining an airborne platform is more expensive than a terrestrial mast. The most effective HAPs platform is the one that can provide much greater coverage than terrestrial cells at a cost less than a few terrestrial cells. Different HAPs platform providers are competing on the basis that they have the lowest cost technology.

For the UK, a tethered balloon, flying at a few hundred metres to a 1.5 km up, might be most effective. Such a balloon could stay airborne for many years, with short maintenance sessions every few months where the balloon is pulled back down, the antenna is serviced, and its helium is replenished. It might achieve a coverage of about 20-50km radius, depending on population density replacing something like 100 or more conventional cells. It could host multiple 5G base stations, using beam-forming antennas to deliver significant capacity. Of course, there are challenges, predominantly associated with planning permission but local benefits could be offered so rural communities might welcome installations, furthermore the precise siting requirements of conventional masts are removed if typical ranges are 20 to 50 km. Positioning also needs to avoid commercial airports and respect airspace change management procedures, but these issues ought to be soluble.

Delivering truly ubiquitous coverage across the UK might require something in the region of 20,000 additional conventional cell towers per network. Rural towers tend to be expensive – perhaps costing around £250k each on average, depending on just how rural they are. Planning permissions take time, no network operator in the UK has ever achieved a build rate of more than 1,000 rural towers per year. Such a network deployment programme, then, could cost as much as £10 billion assuming two networks for the UK shared between three or four operators but would likely take decades. But much of this could be replaced by a few hundred tethered balloon HAPs. Each of these might be £5 m to £7m, totalling around £1 billion. While there will still be a need for more terrestrial sites, especially in smaller urban areas that need infill, such an approach could reduce the cost of ubiquitous coverage massively.

Satellite systems providing terrestrial coverage have been present for decades, with Iridium providing coverage to bespoke handsets and more recently Starlink providing high data rate broadband connections and Apple enabling "direct to handset" (DTH) emergency calling on iPhones. Many companies including SpaceX, Kuiper and others are working on satellite systems that can provide direct to handset (DTH) services that go beyond the iPhone emergency messaging and aim to deliver at least GSM-level service.

The key advantage of satellites is truly ubiquitous coverage outdoors (satellites tend not to work well indoors because the signal is attenuated by the building roof). Satellites could provide the final resource where terrestrial and HAPs systems are not viable. Their weakness is their low data capacity and higher latency[30].

Hence, through a mix of conventional cells, HAPs, and satellite systems (an integrated network of networks), ubiquitous coverage might eventually prove an order of magnitude less expensive that currently envisaged using cell towers alone.

There is a possibility, even a likelihood, that, with so many LEO satellite constellations being launched, some owners will act strategically to see off competitors by flooding the market with capacity prices well below cost. This would severely tempt MNOs to reign back on investment in upgrading their terrestrial networks to save money. The government has a role to play to ensure the UK does not finish up with a significant part of its rural mobile infrastructure dependent on "high risk" owners based outside of the UK's jurisdiction who may then increase the price once they have eliminated competition.

9.3.4.3    Leave one slimmed down GSM network running

MNOs would mostly prefer to shut down the older networks as this reduces the cost of maintaining the equipment and software, the amount of electricity consumed, and allows the spectrum used to be refarmed to more spectrally efficient newer generations. Most have already turned off 3G. However, 2G is proving harder as there are many devices, often machines and sensors such as smart meters, which are not 4G or 5G capable and so would lose connectivity were 2G turned off. To help the process the UK Government has made a policy decision that 2G networks should be turned off around 2033 signalling to end-users that they need to replace equipment by this time and helping alleviate the risk to MNOs that they suffer adverse publicity should a switch-off result in a harmful outcome.

---

[30] Satellite latency is typically high compared to a terrestrial 5G link. However, if the connection needed is trans-continental, then satellite latency can actually be lower than terrestrial connectivity as the speed of light in space is higher than that in fibre optic cables such as under-sea cables.

Costs are hard to come by, but it seems likely that MNOs could save £m's a year by turning off 2G earlier. However, the cost of retrofitting those smart meters that are not 4G compatible could be £bn's. A way to help reduce MNO costs while avoiding the retrofit costs would be to modify the policy decision to close all the GSM networks around 2033. Instead leave a single thin GSM network running on just 5 MHz to support the tens of millions of "things" currently attached the GSM networks and close down all the others sooner. This saves money for the operators closing down early and saves money for the Government by preventing early change-out of smart meters and similar, part of which can be used to compensate the operator still running a GSM network. The Government could compensate the MNO running the single network from the "savings" from avoiding early retrofit.

Forcing a change-out now could lead to many of these "things" migrating onto 4G networks. But it is highly likely that 4G technology will eventually be changed out to 5G technology. A specific feature of 5G is the ability to handle traffic from a vast number of "things". But 5G chipsets will be too expensive for quite some time for very low cost "things" applications. Requiring the close down of GSM networks too soon may be driving many to incur the cost of a double change-out.

In addition, leaving the thin GSM network running provides another layer of network resilience.

### 9.3.4.4    Energy costs

There is, quite rightly, strong drivers to reduce the energy consumption of mobile networks. These efforts are all along the lines of doing the same thing but in ways that use less energy and at broadly the same cost. Some of the concepts we have suggested earlier fall into this category. For example:

- Off-loading traffic to Wi-Fi or other networks reduces the number of carriers needed.
- HAPs may prove to be more energy efficient than multiple, generally underused, rural base stations.

What comes next falls into a category of substantial investments being needed to reduce the carbon footprint of mobile infrastructures. Provisioning substantial battery capacity at every base station fed by local renewable power sources (solar and wind) could generate substantial carbon savings. But, as has been shown earlier, there is already a substantial investment deficit in meeting existing highly desirable essential quality of coverage improvements.

Beyond that come the difficult choices for carbon savings. Much energy could be saved with a single mobile network operator monopoly, but this will likely have an adverse impact on consumer choice and prices. Ever higher data speeds result in more energy consumption but deliver greater quality pictures and new experiences. Implementing network functions in software diversifies vendor supply but will consume more power than dedicated integrated circuits. These choices are political in nature and falling to a government to make.

What the Government needs to avoid is having its net zero policy goal relying on pushing up energy costs driving directly against its mobile infrastructure policy goal whose success depends upon driving down infrastructure running costs, of which energy costs are a significant part.

Meanwhile MNOs and system vendors are already doing a great job in driving more energy efficient networks. This could be facilitated by the Government not only making more efficient mobile networks a part of the national 6G vision (alongside delivering better universal high quality mobile coverage) but giving it substance in research funding priorities.

9.3.4.5    Reducing base station deployment costs

Anything that can cut the cost of a base station or backhaul to make cell splitting cheaper helps drive up spectrum efficiency. Possible approaches include:

- Rights to attach antennas on public or other utility infrastructure free of charge.
- Free aerial attachment rights to every lamp post (a dream of every visionary radio engineer for the past 50 years).
- Right to tap into fibre runs that have received any significant public subsidy.

These examples are not currently within the gift of Ofcom but could be enabled by the Government, giving Ofcom the best regulatory tools for a new age of challenges.

### 9.3.5    In summary

In Economic Zone 2 there are valuable economic and societal gains to be achieved by creating the pro-investment conditions for significantly extending the essential quality of coverage.

*Conclusion: What all the above illustrative examples have set out to show is that Ofcom can re-purpose its spectrum and telecoms policy tools to quite dramatically transform the business case to make the investments needed viable. The quest is getting far more extensive essential quality of coverage for far less money.*

The list, summarised below, is unfiltered to show the breadth of possibilities. The stronger ones have very promising possibilities, and the weaker ones may provoke the lateral thinkers to come up with something better in that space.

*Conclusion: Our new approach to licensed mobile spectrum policy makes "cooperative dynamics" one of its pillars in an overlap of political, regulatory, and industrial power. Focussed narrowly on infrastructure quality of coverage, it creates the structure and conditions to give life to transformative ideas and the widest reach from whence those ideas can come.*

| **Example initiatives that could make near-ubiquitous coverage viable** |
|---|
| *Find new revenue streams:* |
| 1. Repurposing annual licence fees to invest in required coverage |
| 2. National roaming as a profitable premium service |
| 3. Charging large content provider a carriage fee |
| 4. Catalysing power of public procurement |
| *Exchange of new spectrum for new commitments* |
| 5. 600 MHz from DTT to mobile post 2034 |
| 6. 600 MHz earlier migration |
| 7. New mid band spectrum (for 6G?) |
| *Secure much greater efficiency gains* |
| 8. Pooling of spectrum |
| 9. Relocate selected towers to fill cell edges |
| 10. Antenna improvements |
| 11. UHF bands defragmentation |
| 12. Transitioning UHF FDD to TDD |
| 13. Network-driven roaming |
| 14. Cell sweeping technology |
| 15. Large intelligent surfaces |
| 16. AI and machine learning optimisation |
| *Cut infrastructure costs* |
| 17. Market expansion model that aggregates small initiatives |
| 18. Greater Wi-Fi traffic off-loading and coverage extensions |
| 19. Use tethered balloons to lower cost of more rural coverage |
| 20. Integrating next generation LEO coverage |
| 21. Leave one "thin" GSM network to cut massive IoT transition costs |
| 22. Lower energy costs by aligning net zero and mobile infrastructure goals |
| 23. Regulate free aerial attachment rights to public/utility facilities |
| 24. Regulate free aerial attachment rights on every streetlight |
| 25. Regulate low cost backhaul over taxpayer subsidised rural fibres |

## 9.4 Economic Zone 3 –Where there is a societal case for improving the essential quality of mobile coverage

The goal for any government for a critical national mobile infrastructure is that it should benefit everyone in all corners of the United Kingdon. There should be no "left behind" areas. The fact that the nation's finances may be in a poor state today may lead to a pause in the delivery of that ideal. But it should remain a goal that it will eventually get delivered. This will motivate the research community to look ahead at what a Shared Rural Network 2.0 and 3.0 might look like. Research could lead to innovations that make that goal happen sooner. The delay may turn out to have been a blessing in disguise in terms of a better end result of essential quality of coverage at a lower cost using better technologies.

### 9.4.1 Shared Rural Network 2.0

The long-term solution for the most deeply rural areas is likely to come with the next generation of Low Earth Orbiting satellites with more powerful antenna arrays. In the less deeply rural areas lower cost alternatives to mobile towers can bring incremental improvements. As introduced earlier in Section 9.3.4.2, tethered balloons look worth considering. The advantages of a tethered balloon are:

- Antenna heights can be adjustable up to 1 km.
- Latency will be lower than that from LEOs.
- Transmitter powers will be lower.
- Less rain fade margins needed.
- No problematic international orbit coordination needed.
- Can be lowered to add improved technology.

### 9.4.2 Shared Rural Network 3.0

The great thing about LEO satellites is that their antennas are so high above the earth that they can see everywhere and cover everywhere (at least where there are no obstructions). The downside is that they see too much, spectrum re-use is limited, and this makes them inherently capacity-constrained within a given spectrum. This makes them ideal for covering large remote low traffic areas of a country.

Already the ability to connect a smartphone directly to a commercial low orbiting satellite (LEO) has been demonstrated. But the feasible data speeds limit the use to the equivalent of SMS (short messaging service). Considerably more power can boost the data speed from LEO to the smartphone. But the smartphone power cannot be boosted and stay within safe levels and on top of that bigger batteries would be inconvenient. Higher data speed connectivity to cars is an easier challenge with innovative planar arrays layered on car roofs for example.

The necessary advance is on the satellite antenna systems. They must shape the beam, so all the power arrives at the smartphone and is not spread across the entire visible coverage area. This can be done either with a huge antenna array (or a massively complex one) or getting all the antennas of all the visible LEO satellite passing overhead to act together as if they were a single phased antenna array.

The geopolitical competitive race between the rising number of LEO satellite operators is likely to see the pace of these sorts of innovations speeded up.

*Conclusion: There is an inevitability of Zone 3 coming last in the economic priority pecking order. There are promising developments that can turn this delay into a positive of being able to exploit far more cost-effective approaches to raising the universal essential quality of coverage.*

## 9.5 Flexible regulatory approach across the three zones

Defining the three zones is helpful in changing old thinking that a competitive market in mobile networks would deliver everything and then learning to live with a sub-standard mobile infrastructure when it does not. It also identifies what must change, where and who needs to take responsibility in order for the country to have a much better performing mobile infrastructure. However, the three zones should not be treated as watertight compartments. The boundaries are soft and in practice the benefit of measures taken in one zone will create benefits in another zone. The goal is an essential quality of coverage that is universal.

# 10 Lightly licensed spectrum

## 10.1 Introduction

In this chapter we turn to a different form of licensing often termed light licensing where in most cases all are allowed to access the spectrum but need to register in some format and potentially make some payment to do so. Dynamic spectrum access (DSA), a much-discussed concept, is a form of light licensing and will be covered in the chapter.

Our introduction in Chapter 1 flagged this as being on a promising path. We start here by setting out why light licensing might be needed as a complement to licensed spectrum and then turn to look at ways that it can be implemented. Finally, we consider how extensive its role might be in future spectrum management.

All this will point to the challenge for Ofcom being how to handle the problems of "success". Their consultation on their strategy for the 2020's drew praise for its direction of travel towards the increased use of spectrum sharing and stripping out the currently excessive loading of safety margins upon safety margins. The momentum has been maintained with their November 2023 consultation on "Proposals to enhance our shared access framework to support a growing variety of spectrum users". The only thing we see as missing from the broad strategy is deeper integration between licensed and lightly-licensed strategies.

## 10.2 Where licensing does not work well

Licensing is entirely appropriate for applications such as cellular, although as we have discussed, that licensing of spectrum, particularly that used for a critical national infrastructure, is better performed on a managed basis rather than purely via economic incentives. But there are many areas where licensing has not delivered full utilisation of the spectrum or where its application is highly problematic. These are discussed below.

**Hard to clear**. There are bands that are licensed to users who do not fully use the band but are unwilling to trade their spectrum or directly facilitate usage by others. Often these are governmental users, such as the military or aeronautical. There have been many attempts over the years to prise spectrum back from these users, but results have been disappointing. Directly requiring spectrum to be returned is generally met with a response that the spectrum is needed, is being used, but that all details are confidential so no verification of this is possible. An economic approach based on pricing has been tried in a few countries, including the UK, but Government departments are not driven by profit and most anticipate that should they gain income from selling spectrum or from reducing annual licence fees, that the Treasury will simply apportion this by reducing their annual budget. Hence, financial incentives are weak.

There have been cases where spectrum has been returned or shared, but often these result from Government intervention requiring bodies like the military to return a set amount of spectrum (eg 500MHz) by a given date. This has been backed by requiring them to pay a high spectrum fee where the Treasury game plan is to get them to trade off holding onto unused spectrum or have money to buy new tanks or fighter aircraft. It has sometimes been characterised as "a market approach" but having the Treasury at both ends of the transaction makes it a highly manipulated market. It is also a blunt tool and risks undermining military efficiency if the ambition is set too high.

An alternative is needed which allows the incumbent to keep the spectrum and continue to use it as they need to but allows others to use the spectrum around them in areas where there is no military use, in a way that does not cause interference.

**Mix of licensed and unlicensed**. In some bands there is a desire to mix licensed and unlicensed use. For example, this is currently being debated in the upper 6GHz band where enabling both cellular and Wi-Fi use is seen as potentially advantageous. This is because cellular use is likely to be limited to denser areas whereas Wi-Fi use will be more evenly distributed and generally indoors and hence there is scope for both. Also, the future demand from either is uncertain and hence there is a desire to "allow the market to decide" by enabling both and seeing which application emerges as the most adopted.

Directly allowing unlicensed into a licensed band may cause interference because of the uncoordinated and uncertain use of unlicensed spectrum. Hence, some approach is needed which segregates and arbitrates usage.

**Not incentivised to share**. There are some uses where the incumbent could share but has no clear incentive to do so. An example is the terrestrial broadcast TV system, where there is much "white space" in areas where most TV channels are not transmitted. But the broadcasters are often only weakly associated with the transmission network owner, and it is unclear how any costs or gains from sharing would be distributed. Also, such bodies are often risk-averse and so disinclined to agree to anything that might compromise their service. So, while, in principle, the licence holder could directly allow others to share their spectrum, in practice they are unlikely to do so.

Regulatory intervention, using a method like that in the "hard to clear" category is needed.

## 10.3 Where unlicensed does not work well

Unlicensed use works well where there is little interference between users. But as the potential for interference grows then congestion increases leading to the risk of a "tragedy of the commons" where there is so much interference that the spectrum becomes useless to all (although the protocols in systems like Wi-Fi tend to prevent complete meltdown). The risk of interference is correlated with the transmission range of the unlicensed use. Solutions that are restricted to a home, or even a room within a home, are unlikely to interfere with others, and even if they do, the solution is within the control of one person or household who can resolve it. Solutions that spill out well beyond the home and into the homes of others are much more problematic.

Unlicensed solutions aim to avoid excessive interference mostly through restricting the power levels allowed. But in some cases, there are other restrictions. For example, in some Wi-Fi bands only indoor routers are allowed – this is enforced by not allowing weather-proof routers to be sold. Higher power Wi-Fi systems are only allowed if they are under database control - effectively a form of light licensing.

This highlights the fact that there is a continuum of optimal solutions from unlicensed through lightly licensed and ending in licensed depending on a range of factors but often primarily the potential for interference. Wi-Fi solutions in 6GHz are available fully unlicensed for indoor lower power use, and lightly licensed for outdoor and higher power use. Lightly licensed, then, is effectively an extension of unlicensed use where the potential for interference is too great for unlicensed use to work well.

In a similar way, unlicensed spectrum cannot provide any guarantees of freedom from interference since more users might enter the spectrum at any point. But some users of technologies such as Wi-Fi would value a quality of service (QoS) guarantee, for example if they rely on their Wi-Fi network as part of their business operation.

In this case, it may be appropriate to limit the number of unlicensed users in some way to protect QoS. Light licensing using controlled entry to the band can achieve this.

## *10.4 How to achieve light licensing*

Light licensing is a form of control of usage. It differs from licensing where the regulator has little control over usage, and instead the licence holder controls their own usage in the manner that suits them best. It differs from unlicensed where there is no control over usage other than indirectly through terms such as limiting transmitter power.

The aim is to have the minimum control needed to achieve the objective, which is normally controlling interference to other users.

Attempts have been made to fully decentralise this control, for example by having devices sense whether there is incumbent use, and only access the spectrum is they do not detect other usage. This approach is used, in part, in the Citizen Broadband Radio System (CBRS) scheme discussed below. Indeed, sensing is also used in unlicensed spectrum by some technologies such as Wi-Fi to prevent self-interference, but this is typically a technological choice rather than a regulatory requirement.

However, sensing is an imperfect solution. There is a risk that the device doing the sensing does not hear nearby emissions. That may be because it is in a location where the signal is blocked, perhaps by a building or similar. Or it may be because the emissions are hard to detect. Hence, there is a risk that interference is caused due to what is known as the "hidden transmitter" problem. Further, sensing tends to add complexity to devices, increasing their cost.

A better alternative is often known as the database solution. A database, perhaps owned by the regulator, or a body approved by them, contains information about the incumbent user or any users that need protection. This may be the location of broadcast transmitters or of ships using radar. The information may be relatively static or rapidly changing as transmitters move. Regardless, the database needs to know enough about the usage to be able to protect it.

A device wishing to access the spectrum then contacts the database (without using the spectrum band that is lightly licensed) and provides information such as its location and desired power levels. The database can then use propagation models to predict whether that usage would interfere with known incumbent usage and authorise the applicant accordingly. All light licensing databases have this general structure, but they can differ dramatically in the mechanisms for validating entry into the band. There can be one or multiple databases – for example CBRS has multiple commercial database providers who coordinate between themselves. It may also be possible to reduce the oversight needed by using tools like blockchain to provide verification of transaction, although there are also downsides associated with the speed and energy needed for these concepts.

In principle, a licence holder could implement their own database solution and open access to their band to others. They might wish to charge for this access to have an incentive to do so. Concepts of the military doing this and allowing shared entry by a small number of cellular operators were proposed around 2005 under the name licensed shared access (LSA), but it was never implemented, likely for the reasons set out earlier – that Government users are not driven by profit. Also, such users may lack the knowledge to implement such a database.

Hence, it generally falls to the regulator to establish and manage a light licensing scheme.

## 10.5 Light licensing is infinitely flexible

The rules of entry into light licensed spectrum can be simple or complex. Experience has shown that databases allow inventiveness in delivering highly flexible solutions. Such solutions can also be changed at short notice if needs be. It seems likely that databases could be used to deal with any imaginable situation with sufficient ingenuity.

This can be illustrated with a range of examples. There are detailed case studies available on most of these, the aim here is only to illustrate how light licensing can work and its flexibility.

**TV white space**. One of the earliest database-driven schemes dating back to around 2010 allowed the use of relatively low-power transmissions in UHF terrestrial TV bands where particular TV channels were not in use. TV usage was entered into a database and then applications for entry tested against whether interference might be caused to TV receivers. In the US approach a simple "yes/no" decision was returned, whereas in the UK approach a maximum allowed power level was returned providing increased flexibility. No protection between unlicensed users was provided.

TV White Space (TVWS) was relatively simple. TV usage rarely changes, and TV transmissions are uni-directional. However, TVWS failed to gain traction partly because of a concern that the TV spectrum would be refarmed to cellular, removing the white space, and partly because only a few regulators were willing to go ahead with the regulatory change and database implementation, so economies of scale were never reached.

**CBRS**. A more recent approach, developed around 2016 in the US but only implemented commercially since around 2020, is the Citizen Broadband Radio System (CBRS). This allows sharing of spectrum used by the US navy for ship-borne radars for commercial and individual cellular usage.

A key difference with TV White Space (TVWS) was the "multi-tier approach". The incumbent (the US navy) has complete protection from interference. At the next level, access rights were auctioned in relatively small geographical areas. Those who acquired these rights, known as Priority Access Licences (PALs), can use the spectrum if there is no naval use, and are guaranteed protection from interference from other non-naval users. Priority Access Licenses have many of the elements of licences in that they were auctioned and provide certain rights, but Priority Access Licenses can only be used where the incumbent is not present. Priority Access Licences were generally acquired by mobile operators and cable operators to deliver a commercial service.

The lowest tier is termed General Authorised Access (GAA) and is close to TV White Space (TVWS). Any user can request access without needing to make a payment but only if it will not cause interference to the incumbent and to the Priority Access Licence holders. GAA users have no protection from other users and hence this tier is akin to unlicensed access but with a need to first gain authorisation.

We do not necessarily advocate exactly this approach and have concerns about the use of the wrong sort of auctions as discussed in Part 1, but this approach shows that light licensing can have multiple different types of access or users within a band with different rules of access for each.

There is one other issue. The US navy declined to provide the location of its usage (its ships). Instead, sensing must be used to detect whether there are ships nearby. Database operators deploy a dedicated set of sensors, often along coastlines, that feeds into their database. This is highly inefficient. The sensors are both expensive and imperfect. The need to continuously sense means others cannot use spectrum nearby as it would deafen the sensors. It would have been far better had the navy been willing to directly update the database – after all they ought to know where their ships are[31].

---

[31] One way to do this would be to have a spectrum usage database inside the DoD notional security fence, staffed by defense officials and commercial user engineers, all of them having the necessary security clearance. This can then provide desensitised data to the commercial database providers.

**Upper 6GHz**. This is not a solution that has been implemented but is being considered. As mentioned earlier, there is debate as to whether the upper 6GHz should be unlicensed to allow Wi-Fi usage or licensed to allow for cellular usage.

It might be anticipated that the mobile network operators (MNOs) would deploy 6GHz only in the most congested areas. In other areas lower frequency bands would be preferred. Areas for MNO deployment are likely to be city centres, key transport hubs and similar. MNOs might deploy an outdoor network of 6GHz cells across the centre of the largest cities.

Conversely, the key need for additional Wi-Fi bandwidth might be distributed across homes, offices, and factories across the country, many of which will not be in city centres.

In places like stadiums, where there can be a high demand for data, it may not matter to the attendees whether the spectrum is used by Wi-Fi or cellular as it is likely that their devices could access either. Hence, cellular or Wi-Fi, or a mix, might be deployed depending on the preference of the venue owner and the MNOs.

It would clearly be beneficial to allow both types of usage:

- MNOs would be able to use the spectrum in the congested areas where they need it. But such congested areas might only be 1-5% of the country.
- Wi-Fi users would have full access to the band in all the remaining areas, perhaps 95-99% of the country, and partial access in the other 1-5%.

Those wanting to self-deploy would be able to do so on their premises, perhaps using nearly all the spectrum if they are not in dense urban areas. This is a far better outcome than either cellular or Wi-Fi, but not both, having access.

To illustrate the flexibility of light licensing and databases we illustrate one possible approach to cellular/Wi-Fi sharing.

Anyone wishing to use the band must register each base station with a database. So, for example:

- MNOs would register each base station prior to deployment and only deploy if a spectrum assignment was provided. However, they could, for example, register base stations for a complete city deployment simultaneously, adjust their plans as needed depending on the authorisations allowed, then roll out over a period of time.
- Private cellular deployments (eg 5G in a factory) could register their base station and then deploy, gaining the ability to self-deploy networks in these bands.
- Users with Wi-Fi routers would install their router. This would be able to work in the 5GHz and lower 6GHz band and would determine what authorisation was available to also work in the upper 6GHz band.

Authorisations would be for extended time periods – for example up to 10 years – to allow sufficient certainty for MNOs to deploy infrastructure.

The spectrum can be divided among a range of users, but with more available where not all users wish to access it. For example, if there were 720MHz in the upper 6GHz band, then this might be divided as 320MHz for Wi-Fi and 100MHz each for up to four MNOs or private cellular networks. These are minimum numbers. For example, the first applicant in an area might be an MNO that might request 500MHz. This would be granted. However, if a Wi-Fi request was subsequently received then the 500MHz allocation would be reduced to 400MHz and the Wi-Fi user granted 320MHz. If another MNO then requests say 400MHz, each MNO would be granted 200MHz. The size of the allocation would reduce as needed but never below the minimum guaranteed level. (If subsequent requests are made that would require such a reduction, then these requests are refused.)

Where multiple requests are made from the same entity, eg an MNO, then interference between these requests is not evaluated – it is assumed that the MNO will manage their own allocation to avoid self-interference.

Rules are required to prevent entities accessing more spectrum than needed or attempting to forestall competition. There could be a "use it or lose it" provision that any assignment must be used within a set period (eg 12 months) of making the assignment. This could be verified with data sent from the base stations or Wi-Fi access points to the database showing the amount of user traffic carried per day or similar. Entities that have high numbers of lost assignments might be barred from making further assignment requests.

While this approach has not been implemented it shows the flexibility of light licensing and databases. There are of course other possible approaches Ofcom will be considering.

## 10.6  Future potential

Database systems are limited by the accuracy of their propagation modelling. If the model is inaccurate then either uses are prevented that could have been allowed, or interference is caused. Generally, it is the former since it is regulators who set the rules and they tend to be risk averse, driven by users demanding no interference under any circumstances.

There are emerging approaches for improving modelling. For example, cellular handsets constantly measure signal levels from cellular and Wi-Fi networks. The location of most Wi-Fi networks has been catalogued by entities such as Google. Handsets measurements will often show a strong Wi-Fi signal and a weak cellular signal when inside a building, and the converse when outside. The difference between the inside and outside measurements is the building penetration loss. Using a large number of measurements, crowd-sourced from handsets, could allow each building to be "finger-printed" with specific data on its key radio parameters. That would then allow greater indoor use in buildings with large penetration loss, even when close to other shared users. Similar approaches can be used to fine-tune other propagation models with specific corrections where they are in error. Where there are insufficient measurements, use of machine learning can help with better estimates.

Another approach is to monitor when interference does occur and then modify the database rules. That allows for greater risk taking since the implications of interference are much less. This can be achieved with incumbent receivers that can signal when they are receiving interference. For example, TV receivers can assess when they have a high signal level but also a high error rate. They can then use their broadband connection (eg their connection to the home Wi-Fi) to return this information to the database. Such feedback is extremely powerful and could lead to much higher spectrum utilisation as well as much greater certainty of QoS. There are so many possibilities.

## 10.7 A major initiative – sharing all defence spectrum

In the UK, the Ministry of Defence (MoD) put forward a proposition that all defence spectrum – which then comprises in the region of 50% of all spectrum – could all be shared[32]. A database solution would be used, as set out above, with access allowed where it would not cause interference with defence usage.

This could be a huge win. Intuitively it seems likely that much of the defence spectrum is lightly used – only in a few geographical areas, which tend to be rural, and often only for a small period such as when a training exercise is underway. Shared access to all this spectrum could be a dramatic step change increase in overall spectrum availability.

The MoD's proposition came with a caveat. They would need to own the database and to set the rules. This is because of the confidentiality of their usage. By owning the database, they could keep usage secret and by setting the rules could be assured that their use would be protected.

This felt like an offer too good to refuse. But Ofcom did refuse it. Perhaps it was an idea before its time and now is the time to re-explore its potential.

Sharing all the military spectrum, indeed perhaps all governmental spectrum, could be the biggest win in spectrum management for decades. This could be the most important initiative for all regulators. Setting up databases is easily done reusing those already developed for CBRS and similar. Developing sharing rules can be quickly done with rules refined over time using the approaches set out above. It would be truly transformational. And it would mean that more spectrum

---

[32]   See   https://www.techuk.org/resource/summary-uk-spf-session-on-pssr-sharing-defence-spectrum.html although the actual presentation is no longer available.

was database managed than not. The regulator that seizes this opportunity could be truly world leading (See our glimpse into the far future in Section 12.5).

## 10.8 The future for lightly licensed spectrum

*Conclusion: It seems likely that light licensing will grow over time as spectrum becomes more congested. Indeed, this may become the primary tool for regulators to change use and enable new types of users.*

Finally, given the topic of this book, it is worth asking whether light licensing is a form of economic spectrum management. Broadly not. It does not involve licensing, trading, or pricing. Rules are set by regulators and not by "the market". However, as the examples have shown there are ways within light licensing where auctions can be used (CBRS) and pricing can be a way of rationing demand if needed. Some approaches (6GHz) do let the market decide, but this is not economical driven. It is, however, highly flexible, enables innovation and appears to be an important tool for future spectrum management. It is good to see Ofcom driving this forward with purpose.

# 11 Unlicensed spectrum

## 11.1 Introduction

Unlicensed spectrum[33] is – as the name suggests – spectrum where users do not need a licence to transmit. The equipment that can be used is subject to various restrictions invariably on maximum power, and sometimes on other aspects such as duty cycle and transmitter height.

While there is a very wide range of applications, unlicensed is broadly needed where individuals own both ends of a link. This is the case, for example, for a Bluetooth headphone. Getting a licence for each user and for each use would be hugely onerous. Using a light licensing approach might not work if there was no way of contacting the database (eg if the phone was not connected to a network). Unlicensed works well, especially where uses are very low power and short range and hence have limited potential to interfere with other uses.

The unlicensed use of most relevance to licensed mobile spectrum use is Wi-Fi. This now plays a major role in the MNOs being able to offload traffic from their more bandwidth constrained networks.

## 11.2 Management of unlicensed spectrum

For regulators there are two key decisions related to unlicensed spectrum:

- How much spectrum to make unlicensed.
- What rules should be used to manage an unlicensed band.

Decisions on the amount of spectrum are difficult. It is hard do this using economics since millions of individual users cannot participate in auctions or

---

[33] Unlicensed spectrum is more correctly termed "licence exempt spectrum" but we adopt the more commonly used term here.

easily signal their use and requirements[34]. In some cases, it may be possible to let licensed and unlicensed users battle it out, with the market deciding, as in the 6GHz example in the previous chapter, but this can only work if the unlicensed use is able to access a database – at 6GHz Wi-Fi routers are able to do so using their backhaul link.

In principle, regulators could try to predict the Gross Domestic Product (GDP) impact of dedicating a band to unlicensed use compared to other potential uses and then select the option that maximises GDP. But in practice, determining the GDP contribution of unlicensed usage is very difficult since there is typically limited data about how much it is being used, and few price signals such as monthly subscription fees. Previous attempts to determine the economic value of Wi-Fi have been inventive but led to widely varying results, not inspiring confidence in accuracy. Predicting the future usage over a decade or more is also highly uncertain. Managing spectrum by predicted GDP impact is likely to favour existing licensed solutions for which there is good data and for which usage is easier to predict. It is likely to penalise innovative new uses that do not exist and for which forecasting is very hard. This does not appear to be a good approach.

In practice, regulators tend to subjectively assess whether there is likely to be high levels of demand for a particular unlicensed service. If there is limited licensed demand for the same spectrum, then the decision becomes relatively easy.

We discuss whether there might be better ways to decide on the right amount of unlicensed spectrum in the next section.

In terms of rules, this area is generally easier. Modelling or similar can provide good guidance as to power levels that can be allowed. Designers of unlicensed technologies can help by designing "polite protocols" into their standards which will aim to avoid interfering with other nearby users and may be able to coordinate with them.

---

[34] There have been attempts for companies to buy the spectrum and offer a "private commons" – allowing for example devices they have made to operate within the band. But none of these have proven successful.

There could be improvements. Rules could be made more dynamic, with devices periodically downloading new sets of rules, perhaps on occasions where the devices had contact with a wide area network or with a device like a handset that could in turn download the new rules. Changing the rules could allow for fine-tuning as more insight was gained from use of the band. Rules could also be location-specific for devices that were able to know their location. Unlicensed devices could also monitor their environment and provide crowd-sourced data to regulators on whether interference was growing, giving regulators greater insight into whether new bands are needed, or rules need to be adapted.

Happily, unlicensed spectrum tends to work well, supporting a wide range of different uses which can deliver high QoS in most cases.

## 11.3  Super forecasters

Deciding on whether to make spectrum unlicensed is a judgement call on whether a band will be better for a country if so assigned. That judgement requires an ability to predict the future with good accuracy, to understand what benefits unlicensed and other uses will provide and to factor in political realities and in many cases the chances of international consensus.

As has been researched and documented, there are some individuals who are much better at such forecasting and judgement than others.

A regulator, or group of regulators, could seek to recruit such a panel, based on prior forecasting accuracy and other relevant tests. That panel could then be charged with making recommendations. Panel members would be regularly re-ranked according to more recent forecasts and removed from the panel if their accuracy dropped over time.

This might be a better approach than the current rather random reliance on teams within regulators influenced by key stakeholders who have much inherent self-interest. It would, at least, bring more rigour and focus to such difficult decisions.

## *11.4 Summary*

*Conclusion: Unlicensed spectrum is highly valuable as it can provide substantial capacity and enable a wide range of applications. More could be done to try to seamlessly weave the success of Wi-Fi into the wider public mobile essential quality of coverage solutions. The key challenge for a regulator is deciding how much spectrum should be unlicensed versus licensed. We recommend one approach is to recruit a panel of independent experts with a proven track record of predicting future developments related to spectrum and wireless.*

# 12 The potential of a much better future

## 12.1 A new model to deliver a better performing critical national infrastructure

The UK has already passed through two mobile spectrum policy revolutions:

- Liberalised Command & Control.
- Market approach.

It is now time for a third revolution – Infrastructure Quality Driven. The idea is simple – redefine the most optimal use of the spectrum for the country as seeking *the best infrastructure outcome* meeting the needs of consumers, citizens, society, and the economy *for the spectrum being used.*

One of the recommended features of this new approach is to see ambitious goals being set that are made affordable by stretching the investments over a 20-year period. One of the advantages of entrusting Ofcom with the duty is their independence and stability makes it likely they will still be around in 20 years having, in the meantime, relentless driven the benefits of a higher universal quality of coverage into all corners of the UK.

But there needs to be vigilance on how the economy and society is changing and what is coming over the horizon that can be reflected in periodic reviews.

We conclude our book looking at that far horizon. We have limited our gaze to areas which may have consequences that need to be considered much earlier. These include a future of unlimited demand (or not), extremes of social exclusion, extremes of AI penetration into spectrum management and how one might at least give a perception of infinite supply.

## 12.2 *Will there be a demand for a universal data rate of greater than 10 Mb/s?*

### 12.2.1 Introduction

So far, we have only examined the rise in data demand that will come from moving mobile services from a "best endeavour" to "a guaranteed" minimum universal data rate ie meeting all concurrent demand. We have assumed the ambition to be in the order of 10 Mb/s. But in the recent past the huge pressure to find more licensed spectrum has almost entirely come from the relentless rise in demand from consumers and businesses wanting to do ever more data hungry things and wanting higher data speeds to do it.

Is this a road without end or is there any reason to believe this sort of demand will plateau? The latter would be good news indeed for the spectrum regulator.

Why an answer to this question matters is the exceedingly long lead time to not only find new spectrum but roll out the new capacity on the new spectrum to every part of the UK. Policymakers traditionally wait for concrete evidence before acknowledging the need for action. This stance would inevitably put them behind the curve and will lead to a continuous rise in network congestion. Overcrowded networks not only suppress demand but also fall short in supporting economic growth and societal needs. Furthermore, the extended time required to implement changes means that these detrimental effects can last for years.

This leaves two options. Either being able to track future demand with enough precision that new spectrum (and capacity) arrives just in time or take the way future computer memory chips are planned (of massively overshooting all known demand) in the expectation that industry and society will find all sorts of ways of mopping up the surplus capacity. The latter rather depends upon the assumption that demand is unlimited.

Here we set out two scenarios:

1. The case why demand is likely to plateau.
2. The case why demand may be unlimited.

## 12.2.2 The case why demand is likely to plateau

Since the 1990s cellular has needed significant injections of spectrum on a 10-yearly cycle. The need for more spectrum has been a result of growth in demand, initially in the number of users and then, since 2007, in the data consumed per user. The 10-yearly next generation cycle to meet these demands has been helpfully linked to the introduction of new generations of mobile technology able to handle wider bandwidths. Historically each new generation has required new spectrum because, with the wider bandwidths, there was insufficient spare capacity to be able to re-farm prior generations.

This need required spectrum regulators to identify new bands, clear them of incumbents and then auction the bands. These were all time-consuming activities and much of the resources of the spectrum regulator were focused on cellular spectrum. In passing, apart from the auction element, this was very much a command & control activity with little evidence of market forces or use of economic tools. It was also generally an act of faith that finding more spectrum for cellular was the right things to do and indeed an imperative.

That era may be coming to an end. Growth rates in mobile data usage stayed at about 50%/year from around 2010 to 2020. But they are now falling and in 2022 growth rates were around 20% on average around the world. The trend lines suggest that they will continue to fall, in which case growth might stop altogether before the end of the decade with data use reaching a plateau. Intuitively this makes sense. Video is by far the highest bandwidth application. Once everyone is watching as much video as they want to then demand will level off. Only if a new application emerges that requires even more bandwidth than video will demand growth pick up. With many already spending all their spare time on their phone and most applications, even social media, having a large percentage of video content, we are likely to arrive close to "video satiation".

Also, as explained in the first part, mobile operators found 5G to be a loss-making endeavour and are in no hurry to move to 6G. Many have said that the move to 6G should be a software upgrade only. If there is no hardware update, then there is no ability to use new frequencies. While this is a simplistic assessment, there may be drivers that push 6G towards operating on existing mobile frequencies.

This all adds up to considerable uncertainty as to whether there will be a classic "clear and auction" programme for 6G. Current activity in bands such as the upper 6GHz, as explained in Chapter 10, points to regulators being unsure as to whether it should be dedicated to cellular and looking for ways to share the band with other users (Wi-Fi in this case) in such a way that if cellular demand does not materialise the spectrum is not wasted.

Future spectrum for cellular may not be needed or may need to be assigned in more flexible ways than in the past.

### 12.2.3 The case why demand may be unlimited

Since the beginning of high-capacity cellular mobile systems (1G) there has been a tight relationship between demand over the fixed networks and demand over mobile networks. Whatever we find useful and enjoyable to do at home or in the office we want "mobilised" so we can carry on doing it on the move or in a nomadic lifestyle.

There has only been one moment in mobile history when public mobile data speeds ran faster than public fixed network data speeds. That was in 1991 when GSM offering 9.6 kb/s and fixed wireline connections were just migrating from 2.4 to 4.8 kb/s. Then data speeds over the public fixed networks just took off. The gap just got wider and wider. The fact that certain uses on fixed broadband network cannot now be run over far more bandwidth constrained mobile network is leading to an argument that there is no demand for them. But is that true?

There is a dystopian vision in which, when a child is just old enough to wear a virtual reality headset, they are sat in an armchair for life. Pizzas and coke get delivered on demand. All the world's rich experiences happen in an incredibly vibrant virtual world. That child can grow old and never have to leave their room. If this is the future, the spectrum regulator can look forward to all the licensed mobile spectrum being handed back. But that does not look a plausible future of humanity to anybody but the manufacturers of virtual headsets and virtual content developers.

So as full fibre gets rolled out across the UK with, for all practical purposes, unlimited capacity, we must believe in a future of unlimited growth being needed over mobile networks. We have foreseen earlier that the tens of millions of cars on the roads today will become driverless cars. This is not an "if" but when. And when it does, whatever we find useful and enjoyable to do at home or in the office we will want "mobilised", so we can carry on doing it on the move.

Getting cracking on rolling out of wide bandwidth 5G along every mile of road and rail link to every corner of the UK is probably already behind schedule. And this may need to be followed by 6G in new spectrum bands.

### 12.2.4   The politics of which scenario is the most believable

All governments and regulators like to communicate only good news stories to the public. The advice from a top civil servant to their minister, on which of the two scenarios for the Minister to support, might take one of two forms:

1.   If money is tight, and there are only limited investments to hand and even more limited new spectrum – the good news story is that some experts believe that future demand for more mobile capacity is coming to an end.
2.   If there are better times and there are opportunities to clear new bands for 6G, then the good news story is that this Government and regulator are not only investing boldly for our future but that of our children and grandchildren.

There is more truth in this than many would want to believe.

## 12.3  Social spectrum efficiency

Those who were in at the very beginning of the mobile revolution had the dream that one day everyone would have their own personal mobile phone. Pre-pay mobiles made a huge contribution to moving in this direction. More recent efforts have been made by the Government, Ofcom, and the MNOs to ensure a range of social tariffs to facilitate access by low-income families to mobile communications.

Now it may well be that smartphones have already reach their ultimate penetration limits taking into account those too young or those that adamantly do not want one (refuseniks). However, below the low-income families are those with no incomes and in many cases no homes and it may well be there are significant numbers that have dropped below the radar. But we will never know if penetration has not been well defined, and it is nobody's job to measure and interpret the data. A simple definition could be "social spectrum efficiency". This would record how close the nation comes to 100% mobile inclusion and imply whose job it is to monitor this.

Why this matters is that the world is moving towards the digitalisation of nearly all facets of the economy and society. This will inevitably raise the consequences of "mobile" exclusion, for example, not receiving the cell broadcast of an impending life-threatening local extreme weather event.

## 12.4  An AI driven spectrum management world

Already machine learning technology is being applied in various parts of mobile networks sub systems. We can already see its use at the component level, for example in massive MiMo antenna systems. As it creeps into various other sub systems researchers are already turning their attention to how this can be orchestrated on an end-to-end basis. After all it makes no sense to be optimising one sub-system if it is at the expense of a sub-optimal performance of another. The outcome will be a distributed Artificial Intelligence machine that will reach deeply into not only how the networks are performing, but how spectrum is being deployed in real time. We are already nearly there at the spectrum end of the MNO's business in how mobile spectrum bands of various capacities and range are being optimised to meet the varying demands of customers on the move.

We have set out the large spectrum efficiency gains possible through MNO's cooperating in bringing into use each other's unused spectrum and getting customers located far out from one MNO's tower handed over to another MNO with a much nearer tower. This is speculative on our part but looks a possibility for local large leaps in capacity when prospects for clean new spectrum bands have dried up. This would draw us towards network resource AI systems working across separately owned mobile networks.

If we then dig deeper into the direction of lightly licensed spectrum, it is on a path of ever greater densification of spectrum sharing. As the complexity of this builds up it will be a prime candidate for progressing use of machine learning and AI to manage and optimise the sharing. As MNO's start reaching into the pool of lightly licensed spectrum to supplement their fully stretched licensed spectrum, the need to manage and optimise resources is now reaching across licensed and unlicensed spectrum and linking spectrum and capacity in order to optimally address demand.

When complexity builds up on this scale and scope the serious threats potentially emerge, not least in AI deciding its own priorities for a scarce natural resource. One of the principles of the new approach we are proposing is that an elected governments sets the goals and rules on priorities. This looks well positioned to allow the UK to embrace the future AI benefits in mobile spectrum management more confidently.

## 12.5  A glimpse at the far end destination

The dream of successive generations of telecommunications research engineers has been to create communications links with unlimited bandwidth. The nearest practical implementation of this has come with fibre optic cables. Mobile research engineers can only marvel at the options fibre optic technology engineers have today for keep adding ever more bandwidth. Efforts by the mobile research community to catch up have involved using ever-higher spectrum bands but these come at a heavy price of ever-higher levels of investment being needed to maintain universal national coverage. The race looks to be a lost cause.

But it is worth finishing this book on a note of greater optimism. An intriguing idea came out of the UK Institute of Engineering and Technology in 2013[35]. The title of their paper was "Demand Attentive Networks - Creating the perception of unlimited bandwidth in an untethered wireless-fibre world". The idea was that if networks could anticipate demand and move spectrum resources around fast enough then users would have the perception of being connected to networks of unlimited bandwidth. It reveals the possible end destination of the current

---

[35] https://www.theiet.org/media/1225/dan.pdf

relentless drive by Ofcom and the industry towards ever greater spectrum efficiency.

A lot of thought was put into this breakthrough idea by the IET Communications Policy Panel members most notably Vodafone's Gavin Young and the University of Surrey 5GIC's Regius Professor Rahim Tafazolli. The critical issues were whether the spectrum could be moved around fast enough, and the demand could be anticipated sufficiently far in advance.

The MNOs are already learning how to move their own spectrum around ever faster to meet their own demand fluctuations. Ofcom is now on an exciting track to achieve the same when their plans for the increased use of spectrum sharing converge with their plans for dynamic spectrum access.

This leaves the research challenge of how much of the spectrum demand can be foreseen in real time. The University of Surrey together with the BBC did a research project taking a vast amount of anonymised iPlayer traffic data and seeing if algorithms could be developed that could have anticipated the second-by-second level of demand. Very respectable figures emerged. O2 produced some fascinating data where, if the MNO knew where the topflight premier league football teams were playing away, a peak demand for data could be tracked from the away team's town to the home match ground and back. This means it can be foreseen. Every operator knows what will happen to local demand when there is a traffic accident on a motorway.

It is surely only a matter of time when large Artificial Intelligence machines (or an Internet of connected AI machines) will be amassing vast amounts of real time data and getting the national spectrum resource pool re-cycled at ever faster velocity, to give every user *the perception* that spectrum was no longer a scarce natural resource...but infinite.

*Conclusion: Our next revolutionary approach to licensed mobile spectrum regulation looks to have the flexibility to embrace a wide variety of future scenarios.*

# 13 The book summarised

The introduction of market forces into spectrum management around the year 2000 appeared a better way of meeting an excess of demand for mobile spectrum for what was then an ever-widening choice of innovative mobile services and technologies. The theory was that this would allow spectrum to flow into the hands of those that would generate the greatest value in its use. Three tools were to be used - spectrum auctions, pricing, and trading - to deliver the most economically efficient use of the spectrum for the country. That has not been how things turned out.

Spectrum trading of licensed mobile spectrum has been so sparce that it contributes very little to economic spectrum efficiency. Spectrum pricing, through annual licence fees, was originally intended as a transitional measure and should have ceased by 2011. Since then, its claimed spectrum efficiency benefits have been as invisible as the emperor's new clothes. The most surprising finding is that, on the balance of evidence, a link between the highest bid price in a spectrum auction and the most economically efficient use of spectrum has never existed in the UK market environment.

The result has been that, for invisible benefits, an extraordinarily high cost has been paid by the industry and the country has been left with a legacy of poor quality of mobile coverage across the UK. An investigation of what went wrong shows two principal reasons. First politicians baulked at the outset and limited the scope of market forces to a sub-scale potential spectrum market. Then the approach was implemented poorly, particularly in how spectrum rights were defined. Taken together the conditions for the market approach to succeed were never created. Second, the world, as it was in 2000, had changed beyond all recognition by 2014. These changes marginalised any possible impact of a market approach.

We show that important elements of what needs to come next are already in place. Licensed mobile spectrum is now inextricably tied into a critical national infrastructure. The economic value from the spectrum flows exclusively through the coverage and capacity the spectrum provides to the mobile access networks.

Therefore, maximising economic spectrum efficiency is now only possible if spectrum policy is focussed on improving the essential quality of coverage of that infrastructure. We set out how a well thought through spectrum policy revolution around "infrastructure quality driven" spectrum management can deliver significant national productivity and societal gains.

A lot of insights are packed into the analysis that may be of interest in their own right, including the impact of driverless cars on mobile network capacity, productive links with lightly licensed and unlicensed spectrum, "cooperative dynamics" picking up where network competition is failing, impact of Artificial Intelligence and rebalancing the policy powers between the government and Ofcom.

The overall insight from the book is that the key to this bright future for the nation's mobile network infrastructure is a new consensus between the government, Ofcom and the MNOs on smarter boundaries between competition, regulation, and cooperation and a shared goal to deliver a guaranteed universal essential quality of coverage all parts of the country will need from our mobile networks over the next twenty years in order to survive and thrive.

# Biographies

## Stephen Temple

Stephen is currently visiting Professor at the University of Surrey 5G/6G IC focusing on mobile technology strategy.

His track record in spectrum began in 1971 when he represented the UK at the ITU 1971 Space Conference on spectrum sharing between earth stations and radio relays. He has since been responsible for two groundbreaking advances in mobile spectrum. He was the first policy maker in the world to bring about the use of a band above 1 GHz for cellular mobile. He was first to propose that 5G could not run on just one spectrum band and came up with the proposal for three 5G pioneer bands, later adopted across Europe. Whilst in the Home Office he planned the change of emergency services radio networks from low to high band VHF.

His past accomplishments have changed the face of the mobile industry. His largest success was as author of the GSM Memorandum of Understanding that was to eventually bring the entire global mobile technology eco-system into lockstep on next generation mobile technical standards. He transformed European technical standards making in helping bring about the European Telecommunications Standards Institute. He was the driving force behind Digital Terrestrial TV and Digital Audio Broadcasting starting in the UK.

In the private sector he pioneered ntl's broadband Internet, harmonised the digital cable TV platforms of merged cable TV companies and become MD of their networks division. He was later director of special projects in Vodafone's HQ Corporate Strategy.

He was awarded a CBE in 1996 for services to trade and industry. He is a Fellow of the Royal Academy of Engineering and the IET. He won the 1994 IEEE prize for international communications and the 1996 GSM Association Chairman's Award for Outstanding Achievement.

**William Webb**

William is CTO of Access Partnership where he provides advice and support to a wide range of clients on matter related to digital technology.

He was one of the founding directors of Neul, a company developing machine-to-machine technologies and networks, which was formed at the start of 2011 and subsequently sold in 2014 for $25m when he became CEO of the Weightless SIG, the standards body developing a new global M2M technology, a position he held until 2019. Prior to this William was a Director at Ofcom where he managed a team providing technical advice and performing research across all areas of Ofcom's regulatory remit. He also led some of the major reviews conducted by Ofcom including the Spectrum Framework Review, the development of Spectrum Usage Rights and cognitive or white space policy. Previously, William worked for a range of communications consultancies in the UK in the fields of hardware design, computer simulation, propagation modelling, spectrum management and strategy development. William also spent three years providing strategic management across Motorola's entire communications portfolio, based in Chicago. He was President of the IET – Europe's largest Professional Engineering body during 2014/15.

William has published 17 books including "The 5G Myth", "Our Digital Future" and "Spectrum Management", over 100 papers, and 18 patents. He is a Fellow of the Royal Academy of Engineering, the IEEE and the IET, a Visiting Professor at Southampton University, and a non-executive director at Motability. He has been awarded three honorary doctorates and the IET's Mountbatten medal, one of its highest honours, in recognition of his contribution to technology entrepreneurship.

# Index

Printed in Great Britain
by Amazon

36229178R00086